On Our Own...Together

Trust Funds for Families with Financially Dependent Loved Ones and Endowment Funds for Small Not-for-Profit and Charitable Organizations

Harry van Bommel

Resources Supporting Family and Community Legacies Inc., Scarborough, Ontario

This book is also available for free reading and printing from our web site at: **www.legacies.ca**

Canadian Cataloguing in Publication Data

van Bommel, Harry
On our own...together:
trusts funds for families with financially dependent loved ones and endowment funds for small not-for-profit and charitable organizations/Harry van Bommel
Includes index.
ISBN 1-55307-005-4
1. Trust and trustees-Canada. 2. Endowments-Canada.
I. Resources Supporting Family and Community Legacies Inc.
II. Title.

KE787.V35 2002 346.7105'9 C2002-901664-9

To contact the author, write or call:

Resources Supporting Family and Community Legacies Inc.
11 Miniot Circle
Scarborough, Ontario
M1K 2K1
CANADA
(416) 264-4665
www.legacies.ca
E-mail: harry@legacies.ca

In memory of our godson, Daniel McGregor, who taught us so much about love, compassion, excitement, joy and acceptance.

In honour of the people who constantly struggle to convince others that everyone, including people with disabilities, need the same basic human supports of: love, food, shelter, friendships, education, work, and most importantly an acceptance of their gifts and love. In testament to those small not-for-profit and charitable groups who are making a real difference in the lives of their communities but who are forced to waste their time and skills on raising operational funds.

Dedicated to Janet, Bram and Joanna who define family and home for me every day as they share in, and support, our work

Table of Contents

Part 4: Resources

What You Must Know First

This book is about methods to secure some financial comfort, or even independence, for (a) your financially dependent loved one or (b) your not-for-profit/charitable organization.

This book is an information guide -- not an instruction manual. The book does not, nor is it intended to offer legal, tax and financial advice. Use it to ask the appropriately qualified people the right questions that fit your specific situation.

This book is really two books in one. **Why does the book combine trusts and endowments together? Why put families with a dependent loved one together with not-for-profit or charitable organizations?**

The answer is their common ground. Although families with dependent loved ones and not-for-profit and charitable organizations have different operational needs and, obviously, different finances, both are involved in trying to secure some financial independence in the future. Both are looking for ways to avoid the monthly and annual contortions of making ends meet. Both have traditionally avoided long-term financial thinking because daily demands are too great. Both have exhaustion (physical and mental) as common denominators of trying to balance current needs with all the struggles and fears of long-term financial comfort. By giving common financial and legal information to both audiences, we hope to satisfy a common need with enough flexibility to meet your requirements.

Also, for a growing number of families, future security is based, in large part, upon their membership in a family group. Such groups usually consist of a limited number of families (less than 15) that have joined together in a common vision for emotional and physical support. Some of these groups have become incorporated and have turned their attention to securing future financial support for its membership. The trust fund information may help the individual families of such a group. The endowment information may help the whole group look at securing future support dollars.

Do your homework to save you, and the people who must follow your directions, as much frustration and time as possible. Spend at least as much time planning, deciding and moving ahead with a trust or endowment fund as you would in selecting a new car or career or in buying a new home. The consequences for your loved one or organization can be life affirming or devastating.

Information, statutes, federal and provincial budgets, legal precedents and investment strategies change quickly and often. Remember to talk to professionals with special expertise in trusts and endowments including: a qualified financial and estate planner, a lawyer, a tax consultant and/or similar professionals before signing any documents. You would not buy a house without a lawyer, so get the expert help you need to ensure the future of your child/children or organization. It is worth the peace of mind.

Examples are provided for illustration only -- their accuracy cannot be guaranteed. *Resources Supporting Family and Community Legacies Inc.*, its employees and agents assume no responsibility for errors or omissions or for damages arising from the use of the published information and suggestions. You must consult with your own professional advisors to decide what is best for your own financial and legal circumstances.

Language and Jargon

A book with financial and legal information always has 'jargon'. The jargon is important to understand if you want to ensure that you and your financial and legal advisors are speaking about the same things. It is just the same as when you learn the jargon when buying a home (e.g., mortgage, deed, conditional sale) or when getting medical help (e.g., oncologist, hypertension, cholesterol). Get a basic understanding from the text and glossary and then get your advisors to help you truly understand the terms and their importance in your specific situation. They learned what the words mean in basic English so they can certainly help you understand them too.

The word ***disability*** is used throughout the book to refer to people who have a developmental and/or physical condition or impairment that limits them performing one or more life functions in a significant way.

Family refers to someone's own biological family as well as to their close friends whom the person includes within their family.

Dependent loved one refers to a person of any age who is somewhat or completely financially dependent on another person, e.g., your child (young or older) with or without disabilities, or a dependent adult (parent, relative or friend).

Small not-for-profit and charitable organizations are those that have operational budgets under $1,000,000 (most of them under $250,000). ***Not-for-profit organizations*** are not charities and can, therefore, not provide an Income Tax Receipt for donations. Both not-for-profit and charitable organizations, however, are governed by a Board of Directors that oversees the organization's mission of providing not-for-profit services, information and assistance. The difference between these two types of organizations is presently under review in Canada.

An ***endowment fund*** is a separate fund of money and/or assets that must be kept for at least 10 years. The interest from the money and assets may be dispersed (a minimum of 4.5% per year) but the principal cannot be touched. Endowment funds can hold money, stocks, mutual funds and bonds, property, and other physical assets. They are usually created to help pay for a specific program or service or to donate to another charitable organization (e.g., a separately incorporated hospital foundation creates and maintains an endowment fund to pay for specific programs in the hospital).

A ***trust fund*** is a method of contributing assets from one person to another with a person in the middle to ensure the money is well spent. One person transfers ownership and control of their contributed assets to a middle person, the ***trustee***, to be held in trust for the benefit of a third person or group of people. The trustee must legally manage the trust in the best interests of the beneficiaries under whatever written instructions given to them by the creators of the trust.

How To Use This Book

Parts 1 and 4 of both the book and the Appendices have common information for families with financially dependent loved ones and for not-for-profit and charitable organizations. Pick out that information that is most relevant to your specific situation. Part 2 of both the content and appendices are just for families and Part 3 for organizations.

Acknowledging the Sponsors

We are truly grateful to **Deohaeko Support Network** for securing a grant from the **Trillium Foundation of Ontario** to provide funding for the research and writing of this book. Deohaeko's commitment to providing information and sharing their own learning with families, not-for-profits and charities is admirable. They practice what they preach with commitment, enthusiasm and good humour. They are a role model to us all.

This book is also available to anyone for free reading and printing from our web site at: **www.legacies.ca** as well as another book on Deohaeko, *We Come Bearing Gifts* by Janet Klees.

Acknowledgements

Deb Thivierge has provided fundamental information, advice and encouragement for this book. Her research and editing skills and her understanding of the fields of both disability and not-for-profit are formidable. I am grateful for her many contributions. This book would not have been possible without her.

I am grateful to the following people and organizations:

ACT (AIDS Committee of Toronto) and **Greg Lichti**, their senior development officer, for help in understanding aspects of creating an endowment fund with a community foundation. ACT has kindly given us permission to reproduce their agreement with the ***Toronto Community Foundation*** as a sample of what a similar agreement may look like for your organization.

Canadian FundRaiser for permission to reproduce part of Jim Hilbourne's article, November 4, 1998 on sample bequest wordings.

Deohaeko family members have provided unending encouragement and support throughout this project. They continue to inspire me with their visionary approaches, their energy and their commitment to providing other families with the same useful information they have collected for themselves. The following members have gone through the book and provided thoughtful feedback for which I am very grateful: Mary and Clive Bennett, Linda Dawe, Helen Dionne, and Harriet Salmers.

Orville Endicott, LLB presented basic starting information to a group of parents on trust funds that was very helpful. His subsequent review of the manuscript helped make the information current and accurate.

Sandra E. Foster gave her kind permission to reproduce two pages from her 1996 edition of *You Can't Take It With You: The Common-Sense Guide to Estate Planning For Canadians* and made useful suggestions during an interview.

Janet Georgieff is the Executive Director of the ***Community Foundation of Durham Region*** and she corrected an error in the section on community foundations.

Alvin Isenberg, M.A. LL.B. gave a thorough review of the material and his extensive, practical revisions have made the material much more useful to the readers.

Jayne Kirby Donahue, LL.B. assisted with information and encouragement early on in this project to give some perspective on trust and endowment funds.

Ronald Hawkshaw, LL.B. is Chairman of the ***Community Foundation of Durham Region*** and provided feedback on the manuscript that was very helpful.

The Heart and Stroke Foundation of Ontario generously permitted us to reprint five examples from their planned giving materials to help illustrate key donation methods.

Colleen Man is a financial advisor whose material helped me grasp the basics of trust and endowment funds. Her encouragement continues to provide support.

James Marshall of ***TD Canada Trust*** for leading me to legal expertise in the field.

Judith McGill did an extensive review of the content from the perspective of a consultant working with families with financially dependent loved ones as well as a journal editor. Her eye for detail has enriched this book.

Margaret E. Rintoul, LL.B. kindly provided up-to-date detailed legal and tax revisions to help make the book as practical as possible. Her background and expertise in this field were most welcome.

We gratefully acknowledge the **Royal Bank of Canada** for permission to reproduce their chart *A Personal and Estate Planning Considerations in Charitable Giving* in our chapter on planned giving.

Lorna Somers generously gave us permission to reproduce the "Sample Endowment Fund Policies" and "Sample Endowment Fund Agreement" from her book *Planned Giving for Canadians.*

Graeme Treeby and **Rodney Dunn** of the ***"Special Needs" Planning Group*** generously permitted us to reproduce their material on discretionary trusts, trustee responsibilities and their life planning format which they use with their clients. These are reproduced in the appendices.

Carol Oliver and **Robert Peacock** of the ***Toronto Community Foundation*** shared information and led us to further sources.

My sincerest thanks and love to **Janet Klees** who models the spirit of this book in every way and who is the primary editor of all of my work. Her suggestions through two revisions of the book have made the final result more readable and useful. She is my inspiration and role model along with our children **Joanna** and **Bram**.

Introduction

Note: This is a short book as you will probably need to read only the half (about 70 pages) that applies to your situation (i.e., as a family member or as an organization). Therefore, we cannot cover every kind of financial situation that relates to your needs. **Adapt the information in this book to meet your needs and use it as a guide to ask the right professionals the proper questions.** There is a lot of specific information out there and professionals and organizations can help you understand the tools and financial instruments you will need to use for your specific circumstances. Look in the recommended resource list at the end of this book and your local library and bookstore for further information.

Sometimes in our quest to know everything about something that is important to us, we get stuck in wanting to read just one last book, visit one more friend who has experience, or attend one more conference or seminar. This is especially true around making financial decisions or writing out our wills. In fact, because we do not want to make a mistake, we often do not make any decisions or we procrastinate in hopes that we won't have to worry about it. Sometimes we procrastinate with the unconscious belief that if we don't write a will, we won't die or if we don't secure the financial future of our dependent child or our organization, someone else will.

This book, then, is about encouraging you to arrange some financial security for your dependent loved one or your not-for-profit/charitable organization.

You, as a family member, must make the legal decisions involved in securing financial comfort or independence for your dependent loved one. If you represent a not-for-profit organization or charity, it is the organization that must make the final decisions about establishing an endowment fund. **You are on your own,** in that sense.

However, **we are together** in trying to make sense of all the financial and legal options out there. We also want to act on this information to secure the futures of our loved ones and our not-for-profit organizations. None of us has to go it alone.

You also have the resources of financial planners, accountants, lawyers and others who can help you make the best decisions possible at the time. This book will provide you with an overview and many of the questions you need to ask to get the best results for your dependent loved one or organization. **You will not make perfect decisions no matter how hard you try.** We cannot predict the future and, therefore, we can only make the best decisions possible given the information and financial/legal circumstances of today. That you are in the process of doing anything at all sets you apart from most families and organizations today.

It is important that you design and act on a thoughtful plan of action during the next 12 months so that you will have some peace of mind for the financial future of your dependent loved one or your not-for-profit or charitable organization. You will continue to review and revise your plans over the coming years but only if you make the all-important decision during the next 12 months to set up your trust or endowment fund.

Sincere Best Wishes,

HARRY VAN BOMMEL

Scarborough, Ontario

Part 1

General Information

Chapter 1
General Information

The following information relates to either a trust or endowment fund. It provides some basic information on trusts and endowments as well as an understanding of how quickly money can accumulate and double through the magic of compound interest.

Briefly, trust and endowment funds are financial methods of saving money and assets for use later on. Rather than being a single account with a trust company, a trust or endowment can be a collection of financial instruments set up 'in-trust'. For example, a trust or endowment fund can include one or more monetary accounts, mutual funds, investment portfolios, land or building ownership, insurance policies, art and other collectibles and more.

Trusts, for our purposes, are set up to provide long-term funds and assets for financially dependent loved ones. These trusts can be used before and/or after the creators of the trust die. In particular, discretionary trusts are established to provide finances to dependent adult children in a way that prevents the loss of government benefits to the child.

Endowment funds are specifically for organizations (not-for-profit and charitable) and are established with a specific goal in mind. This might be the ongoing funding of a specific project or for the long-term viability of the organization's own operational funds. For example, an organization might create an endowment fund to support its home renovation project for families in need or to help cover its own day-to-day expenses including salaries, overhead and services.

Choosing Your Advisors

Nothing is more important in financial planning than choosing your advisors. How do you choose the right ones?

People have different backgrounds, experiences and needs. My accountant may not be the accountant you need. Your lawyer may not be the right lawyer for someone else's family.

First you need to make a list of the things you want this professional to do for you. You will not need a corporate lawyer that specializes in helping companies buy other companies if all you want is a lawyer to write your will and help with your estate when you die. Nor do you want an accountant who has little or no experience in not-for-profit organizations or tax law for endowment funds.

Once you have made your list of needs you can check with your family, friends and colleagues at work for different referrals. You can also call the professional associations of the different groups to ask for a referral to a certified professional in your area.

When you make your first appointment with the person, tell their receptionist that you are looking for a new lawyer/accountant/financial planner and you want to meet them to see if they meet your needs. You should also tell them that since you are not coming for their professional advice, you do not expect to pay a fee for the visit. Make sure that you do not ask for more than a half-hour of their time and that you, in fact, do not spend this free time getting professional advice about your situation. Concentrate on their professional qualifications, abilities and interests.

At the beginning of this appointment, remind the professional that this is a get-acquainted visit at no charge to you. Trust your instinct when you meet the person for the first time. Your first appointment with them is really an opportunity for you to find out if you can talk comfortably with them and whether you feel that they are concerned with your needs, what their expertise is and what fees you can expect to pay. The tone of your questions should be respectful while finding out if this person is the right one for you. Try to determine whether this professional will work with you to meet your financial, legal or medical needs. At the end of the appointment, tell them that you will call them if you decide to use their services.

The following is a list of possible questions you can modify to find out if this is the person you want to entrust with your financial and legal concerns. You will not be able to ask all of the questions. You can find out some of the answers by asking the people who refer you, from their office receptionist or secretary and from degrees and certificates on the wall. Interview several professionals, if possible, before choosing one. You want a working relationship that will last for many years so spending time up front will benefit you in the long run.

You will learn a lot about the person you meet by the way they answer your questions. Although you are the client and, ultimately the person in control, it is rare for professionals to meet people who assert their control throughout the working relationship. Some professionals will be apprehensive and others defensive. Those among them who are confident will be pleasantly surprised and positive about the value of having such an involved, respectful client.

You may also have to decide if it matters to you that the professional shares your moral beliefs and principles. For example, if you want funds invested only in companies that have 'ethical' standards regarding environmental and human rights issues, then your advisor may need to share that interest and make it a priority in researching your investments. If you have a strong need for an advisor who can educate you through the process, then you will need to choose an advisor who values teaching clients as much as getting commissions.

Possible Questions to Ask

1. What is your formal and informal training? How long have you practiced and where?

2. What types of services do you provide? Do you do the type of work I need to get done? *[Show them your list of the work needed and by when.]*

3. Are you flexible with your hours in emergency situations (e.g., explaining financial processes after the death of a spouse)? Can I reach you, or a colleague, 24 hours a day, seven days a week in case of emergency?

4. Will you help me learn more about financial and legal issues related to my situation so that I can become a more knowledgeable consumer?

5. Do you prefer to provide advice and information and help the client make the best decision possible in the situation or do you prefer to work from specific instructions from the client?

6. How do you keep up-to-date in your field and will you provide me with up-to-date information to help me make decisions?

7. Who will take over for you when you are on vacation, ill or near retirement?

8. With what organizations are you affiliated?

9. What is your fee schedule or basis for billing?

10. What options are there, if any regarding your billing?

11. What is the timing of payments?

12. What retainer, if any, is required?

13. Other questions that you come up with:

____

____

The Glossary

It is impossible to write about legal and financial matters without using some of the jargon used by professionals in the field. Professionals have a good understanding of all of these terms so they should also be able to explain them to you. However, it is good if you already have a basic understanding of the terms before you meet with them.

Use the glossary at the end of the book to familiarize yourself with the jargon. Do not try to understand all the terms on first reading. You will see the terms, and their definitions, throughout this book. By the time you finish the book, a quick review of the glossary will help you remember the terms most important for your needs and you will be surprised how much legal and financial jargon you know!

Named Funds Within Your General Fund

Throughout the chapters on trust and endowment funds there will be mention of 'named funds'. The term simply means dividing your trust or endowment fund into smaller funds so that people can have their name attached to their contribution. It is similar to how mutual funds work where there is only one actual fund but administratively it is divided so that each person has a portion of the fund.

For example, a family creating a trust fund for a dependent loved one may decide that named funds could be established within the trust to recognize contributions made by a grandparent, an uncle, two neighbours and the immediate family. A small charity may decide to create different levels of named funds to encourage larger contributions to their endowment fund.

Named funds can be very helpful in raising funds. For example, a donor may want to make a substantial contribution to your fund if you will allow them to name their portion of the fund after them or in honour/memory of a loved one. You might think this an unlikely situation for your trust or endowment fund. Consider, however, someone who has few or no heirs or whose heirs do not need their money. Such a person may have contributed regularly to your organization or the person may be a relative or friend of the person for whom you are establishing a trust fund. Knowing that their name will carry on well into the future and believing that your efforts deserve support may be all the person needs as incentive to contribute.

Organizations such as *Community Foundations* are experts at having many individually named funds within their general fund. They do this in similar ways as mutual funds do in selling units within their funds. (More on Community Foundations later.)

One method, as an example, could be a fund that starts with $10,000 and fund creators decide that each unit in the fund will have an initial unit value of $10. For larger funds, they may decide that each unit will have a value of $100 or $1000. In our example, however, there will be 1,000 initial units valued at $10 each. The next day, Wilma Peters contributes $5,000 to the fund in honour of a parent who has died. She is acknowledged as having contributed 500 units, at $10 each, to the fund. Over the next 12 months the units are invested in a mixed portfolio of equities (shares in companies) and fixed-income instruments (bonds, GICs) and the value of the units fluctuates with market conditions. After 12 months the fund is worth $16,500 (10% increase). At that time each unit is now worth $11 ($16,500/1500 units). Ron Williams now wants to contribute $10,000 to be named after their son who died in the war. His fund is credited with 909.1 units ($10,000/$11).

Keep in mind that this process is administrative; not financial. In other words, the fund is invested as a whole. You are dividing it between named funds and the general, unnamed portion to give people a sense of pride and honour for their contribution and to help them keep track of how their donations are adding to the long-term success of the fund.

The value of each unit can be determined at the beginning of each quarter and contributions that come in during the quarter are added to the fund on the first day of the following quarter. Income (i.e., interest on the principle) distribution between the named funds within your endowment can be done quarterly as well. For example, if distribution of income earned during the quarter is figured out to be 15 cents per unit, then the original named funds would each get $150 (1,000 units x 15 cents); the Peters fund $75 (500 x 15 cents), and the Williams fund $136.37 (909.1 units x 15 cents).

Part 2:

Trusts

Chapter 2
One Family's Story (The Beginning)

The Vivas family (not their real names) includes parents, both aged 54, and two children: Jessie, 21 and Mark, 18. Jessie has a developmental disability. She is able to do many things on her own but requires support to plan her time well, to help with any kind of change in her life, to plan and prepare a healthy diet, and for support in work and community situations. The parents, Susan and Johan are getting older and worried about how Mark and Jessie would live if they should die suddenly.

Susan and Johan have spent a great deal of time and energy to help Jessie live as typical a life as possible. They helped set up a pre-school program at their church when Jessie was very young so that she could play with other children. They fought to include Jessie in the neighbourhood public elementary, and then, secondary schools rather than have her travel by bus to a 'special school' 10 kilometres away from home. They spent many months to finally have Jessie included in the local community centre's programs. They had less trouble getting her into the Guiding program at their local church where people knew Jessie well.

At age 21, Jessie left the secondary school graduating with basic understanding in several subjects. Susan and Johan have juggled support for Jessie to find and keep her part-time job at the mall. This success came through: (a) hiring a person to do one-to-one job support using provincial Ministry dollars, (b) working together with good colleagues at Jessie's job to show them ways they can be helpful to Jessie and vice versa, and (c) getting extra support and encouragement from Mark and a friend who works at the mall. Some of these people have also helped Jessie do some part-time volunteer work at the local provincial park.

Susan and Johan want Jessie to live at home for at least another four or five years. They like to imagine and talk with Jessie about where she might want to live in the future. They are part of a family group that includes other parents who are discussing housing options for their children. This group is also beginning to understand the need and benefit of having a support circle.[1] People who know their son or daughter gather together with the parents and their adult child periodically to help with each child's day-to-day and long-term planning. This group becomes the people that the families can trust to continue on with planning and supporting the individual after the parents become unable to do it themselves or die.

Susan and Johan want to ensure that Mark gets a good start in life and that Jessie is financially independent as much as possible given the family's overall income and assets. They have heard about trust funds through a financial advisor at Susan's work. They know that financial independence is important for both of their children. However, given their work, raising both children, car pooling, Mark's soccer games and practices, time spent with the family group looking at housing options and other family obligations (both Susan and Johan's parents are in their 70s and 80s and require support), they just can't seem to find time to figure out what trust funds are and whether they are suitable for one or both of their children.

---

[1] In Janet Klees' book, *We Come Bearing Gifts*, she describes in greater detail how support circles work including examples of circles at Deohaeko Support Network.

The local Association for Community Living had a session on trust funds for interested parents. Susan took a day off from work to attend and got some basic information to share with Johan later that night. They were referred to several lawyers with some expertise in this matter who charge between $500-$1,000 to prepare a will that will establish such a fund for a family with less than $500,000 in estate assets. The legal fee is a lot of money but Johan likes to work with numbers and figured out that it would work out to only $50.00 a year over the next 20 years to provide his family with some financial security after their deaths and that was well worth the price.

Over the next twelve months they (a) discuss options with their trust company; (b) interview, choose and meet with the lawyer to prepare a will that includes a discretionary trust and prepare Powers of Attorney in case the parents become incapacitated to speak on Jessie's behalf, (c) begin to examine the advantages of creating an *inter vivos* trust while the parents are still alive with a preferred beneficiary election for Jessie, and (d) continue the process of creating a circle of support around Jessie and the whole family. This circle begins the planning work that looks at the non-financial long-term needs within the family and for Jessie after her parents die or become unable to care for her themselves. These four activities take a lot of time and must be fit in with competing demands. However, this process of financial and support circle planning is forcing them to examine what it is they truly believe that Jessie, Mark and they, themselves, need to lead full, enjoyable and relatively, financially secure lives.

In Chapter 7 we examine the results of Susan and Johan's efforts during the twelve months.

Chapter 3
What Are Trusts and Are They for Me?

Trusts are relatively simple to understand and complex to use to their best potential. You will need the expert advice of both a lawyer and tax accountant to make the best choices for your specific circumstances. The following is basic information to provide you with a foundation upon which to make informed choices.

A trust is not a physical thing. Nor is a trust fund usually a single 'fund' at a bank or trust company. A trust is established by a lawyer who draws up a trust deed under each province's trust act. This deed creates a 'legal person' under Canadian law and under the Income Tax Act just as a corporation is considered a 'legal person'. The trust can open up bank accounts, buy property, get a loan, and pay income tax just as all individuals do in Canada.

Trusts are legal and financial tools to permit someone to transfer ownership in real property and other assets (including cash) to a third party for the benefit of a beneficiary. Trusts can accommodate almost any set of circumstances and are limited only by one's imagination and their ability to pay legal and accounting expenses and ongoing trust fees.

A trust can best be explained with an example. Parents of a child with disabilities want to ensure that she is well taken care of financially now and also in the future when the parents have died. They *entrust* some of their present income and assets and/or a portion of their estate to someone else (trustee) who will make sure that the principle and interest of the trust are used in the best interest of their daughter. Therefore, there are three parties to a trust agreement:

1. The parents (called ***settlors***) are the creators of the trust. They can make specific instructions on how the trust is administered and how income and principle must be distributed. Alternatively, they can choose to give the trustee(s) full discretionary powers as to how and when to distribute the trust principle and/or income and how to invest the assets.

2. The ***trustee(s)*** are chosen by the parents and often more than one person is chosen (e.g., 3 can be a good number to ensure some consensus before major decisions are made). The trustee(s) actually receives ownership and control of the assets with the legal requirement that they administer the entrusted assets for the benefit of the daughter. They must follow the directions within the trust as well as instructions provided by a court (if applicable) or provincial statutes. Trustees are usually family members, friends or professionals with some expertise in financial matters and trusts. Professional trustees usually charge a fee based on a percentage of money going into the trust, money taken out and a percentage of the total value of the trust per year. This fee covers the cost of the trustee to manage the trust and distribute income, and when needed, principle from the trust to meet the financial needs of the beneficiary from the trust. The actual fee depends on the size of the trust, the type of distributions, the degree of responsibility the trustee has and the performance of the particular trust. The fees can be 2-3% of funds going in and out plus .5 to 1% of the total value of the fund annually. Check with several professional trustees to get their rates. Trustees who are family members or friends are usually not paid unless the demands of the trust require the person to give up some of their own work time and income.

3. The daughter is the ***beneficiary*** of the trust. There may be directions in place to tell the trustee(s) how to make decisions in the best interest of the daughter plus what to do with the assets in the fund (if any left) after the daughter dies. If the trust is a discretionary trust, it will not have specific directions since the decision-making process is left completely at the discretion of the trustees. Discretionary trusts prevent the loss of government income to beneficiaries of such a trust.

There are different types of trusts but the basic concept is always the same: the parents give something away that they can never get back to a person or organization they trust. Either during their lifetime or after their deaths, that entrusted person or organizations uses the trust to meet their daughter's short and long-term needs. That's it.

Let us look at different types of trust agreements.

Types of Trusts

Trusts are so flexible that they can be quite simple or complex. There are different methods of categorizing trusts and we will look at the key ones. It is not necessary to know all these categories to open a trust fund. However, understanding some of the differences can help you understand the language used by trust companies and others in describing alternatives to you.

To understand the pros and cons of the various types of trusts, you will need to explain your specific situation to your lawyer and tax advisor. What is advantageous to one person would be financially harmful to another.

Trusts created by the parents before death or through their wills are called ***express trusts***. Simply put that means that they created the trusts themselves. All other trusts are created by legislation or courts. For example, assets bequested to minors in a will are put into a trust until they reach a certain age. For that matter, all estate assets are kept in trust until the assets are distributed according to the will and provincial regulations.

Trusts can be created when the parents are alive (***inter vivos trust***) and/or through the parents' will after their death (***testamentary trust***). Income earned in an inter vivos trust may, in certain cases such as with a dependent child, be attributed back to the settlor (therefore, no tax benefit to opening a trust in many cases to shelter assets or make them creditor proof) and may be taxed in the trust at the top marginal taxation rate. That means that for every dollar earned, the trust will pay about 50% in taxes plus professional fees.

For beneficiaries who receive tax credits for mental or physical disabilities, they can get 'preferred beneficiary election' status. This means that their income will be taxed at their own income tax level (often little or no taxes due) and they can keep the income in the trust to accumulate up to their 21st birthday. Other people must have their trust income taxed at the tax bracket of the trust.

There are taxation and lifestyle implications that should be examined before choosing between inter vivos and testamentary trusts. For example, rather than taking out family income now to put into a trust which will diminish what the family can spend on day-to-day or longer-term needs, a testamentary trust or insurance trust established out of an insurance policy may be wiser for life-style and taxation reasons.

Inter-vivos trusts can be used in estate planning as well. They can minimize the income taxes due on death by freezing the value of investments or the shares of a business at the time the trust was created. Check with an estate lawyer and tax advisor to see if this is a useful option in your case. They can also be used to take assets out of public view as trusts are not considered part of a person's estate and, therefore, not part of the public record. This might also decrease probate fees for people with extensive assets. Lastly, these trusts can protect assets from creditors since ownership is transferred to the trust. Again, verify with a lawyer which of these possible advantages may apply to you. If they do not, then a testamentary trust will likely be more suitable.

In some instances, both types of trusts may be appropriate. In other situations, such trusts must be considered in light of other types of legal options so that the appropriate tax, probate fees and methods of controlling financial planning issues can be best determined.

Trusts can be categorized by who is the beneficiary. Testamentary trusts (created by a will) can be specifically for the benefit of: (a) the surviving spouse for the duration of their lifetime (***spousal trusts***); (b) other family members including infant children (***family trusts***); and (c) persons the deceased person thought unable to handle large sums of money (***spendthrift trusts***) or anyone else the person knows. You do not need to be related by blood to create a trust for someone.

Testamentary trusts may be used to defer income taxes and to reduce or minimize income taxes by splitting income between the trust and the beneficiary. Trusts are taxed as if they were an individual for income tax purposes. Any income earned by such a trust is taxed by the same graduated tax scale as personal incomes.

Much effort and planning is required to achieve the required objectives without running into potential pitfalls which can sometimes arise without proper advice.

The Absolute Discretionary Trust

Within the above types of trusts is a particularly-worded trust that may be most beneficial to families with financially dependent loved ones receiving government benefits. The Absolute Discretionary Trust Agreement is a very specific type of trust that can be set up either as an inter vivos or testamentary trust.

The basic feature that differentiates the discretionary trust from other types of trusts is that its special wording gives the trustees absolute and unfettered discretion on how and when to use the funds of the trust. This doesn't mean that they can use the money for purposes other than for the benefit of the financially dependent child but they will decide how much to spend and on what it will be spent. Because of the very special wording of the trust, the Courts in Ontario (Ontario vs. Henson, 1987, E.T.R. 121 Div. Ct.) have decided that "the Absolute Discretionary Trust is not a liquid asset available for the maintenance of the recipient, so Family Benefits should not be cut off." Similar provisions are also available in other provinces now.

Basic Rules About Trusts

For a trust to be valid, it must have 3 things (called the **three certainties**):

1. ***Certainty of intent*** -- a clear intention to create a trust for the benefit of beneficiaries by the settlor in his will or trust indenture or as a result of court order or statute. Ownership must be transferred from the settlor to the trustee and the trustee cannot use the assets for their own use. If the parents retain ownership or the trustee uses the assets for their own benefit, the trust is invalid.

Note: ***Precatory trusts*** are not real trusts. These trusts refer to an agreement where the parents rely on the moral values of another person to do what is right for their daughter but the person has absolute control and ownership of the assets including being able to use it for their own benefit.

2. ***Certainty of subject matter*** -- a clear description of what assets, i.e., income interests (dividends, rental income, interest on principle) and capital interests (property, equities) will be included in the trust. There must be an absolute transfer of ownership to the trust including non-income producing assets such as a coin collection. For example, it is often written in wills that the surviving spouse receives all the assets of the first to die. A different arrangement could be that the husband's assets go into a testamentary trust (upon death) with the wife named as income beneficiary for the duration of her life and his two children the capital beneficiaries. The wife will receive all the income generated by the trust during her lifetime and the children will receive nothing until their mother's death when they will equally share in the capital (principle) remaining in the trust. If drafted

properly, such a spousal trust may defer taxes until the death of the surviving spouse.

3. ***Certainty of objects*** -- a clear description of the beneficiary(ies) of the trust either by name or by class (e.g., 'all of my children'). One may use a class, such as 'all my children' to include children not yet born. A class must be very specific so that it is obvious to the trustee who is included and not included. For example, 'all my close friends' would be difficult for a trustee to decide who is, and is not, a close friend.

Inter vivos trusts are outside a person's estate and, therefore, not held up in probate. There is an advantage, therefore, to create inter vivos trusts rather than testamentary trusts since the trust will continue regardless of the probate process. Other advantages, however, exist for the testamentary trust, therefore get professional advice that best meets your specific needs.

Only inter vivos trusts can be either revocable or irrevocable, i.e., they can be changed or not depending on how the settlor creates the trust. Most inter vivos trusts, however, are irrevocable, which means that the transfer of assets is permanent. This is done for tax purposes. The main advantage for a revocable trust is when the assets transferred will earn little or no income or capital gains. For example, if the parents own some art work, antiques, or other collectibles but worry that the children are not old enough to accept these gifts, they can create a revocable trust which they can cancel at any time when they feel the children are mature enough to appreciate and manage the gifts.

All testamentary trusts, after death, are irrevocable (i.e., the settlor's estate cannot normally revise or collapse the trust). Until people die, however, they can always change their wills and the testamentary trusts.

The terms and conditions of a trust are called ***trust deed*** or ***indenture***. These rules are either written out when the trust is opened while the parents are alive or written out in their will that will create the trust after their death. These rules should include whether the trust can distribute only income earned on the principle (capital) or both. If both, the deed should say whether the trustee has to wait a certain period of time before principle assets can be given to the beneficiary.

There is no minimum amount required to open most trusts. The trust may even borrow funds to avoid attributing the funds to one of the settlors. This may be particular helpful in the cases of trusts for infants, spouses and some arms-length situations (e.g., a trust set up to help a friend).

There is income tax payable on the income generated by the principle in a trust. It is important to know, for income tax purposes, that the income in an inter vivos trust may be taxed at the top taxation rate regardless of the settlor's own tax level if the principle is sufficiently high. If others contribute to a testamentary trust, established by parents, after the parents have died, then the testamentary trust will become an inter vivos trust for taxation purposes and likely charged at the higher tax rate even though the beneficiary is probably at a lower tax bracket.

Beneficiaries can be given a ***life interest*** in property held by the inter vivos or testamentary trust. Life interest, also called ***life tenant***, means the beneficiary receives the right to use a property for a specific period of time (often their lifetime) and upon their death the property title is given to another person. For example, a surviving spouse may have life interest in the family home until her death when it will be transferred to their child (this ***capital interest*** is referred to as ***remainder interest*** and the child as the ***remainder man***).

Discretionary trusts are established by settlors in inter vivos and testamentary trusts to give their trustee partial or complete authority and discretion on how to invest and distribute assets and income within the trust limited only by the powers of trustees as defined by provincial trustee laws and the terms of the trust.

Non-discretionary trusts are established by settlors with clearly defined responsibilities outlined for the trustees including when and how beneficiaries can receive benefits, whether benefits include only income earned or also principle assets, and any specific limitations or requirements as defined by the settlor. For example, the parents may decide that only income earned in the trust can be given to the beneficiary except for the purchase of a home when principle may also be given out.

Multiple trusts by the same settlor for the same beneficiary are deemed to be a single trust. Since trusts are taxed as 'individuals', people have tried to income split by creating several trusts for one beneficiary. The Income Tax Act deems these multiple trusts to be one trust and taxes the income accordingly (usually at a higher taxation rate). However, different people (i.e., maternal grandparents and paternal grandparents) could create separate trusts for their granddaughter and the trusts would not be considered the same but taxed as individual trusts.

One trust for two beneficiaries or two trusts? Sometimes parents with more than one child will want to provide for their children through trusts. The question is whether it is better to have one trust with two beneficiaries or a separate trust for each child. The balance will be between flexibility in asset and income distribution versus tax implications. For example, if a family has two children and the first-deceased parent wants to create a trust for the children they can either:

Option A	Option B
Create 1 trust with 2 beneficiaries.	Create 2 trusts -- one for each beneficiary.
Surviving spouse is trustee.	Surviving spouse is trustee.
Trustee can only distribute income and assets between children to meet personal needs even if distribution not equally divided.	Trustee can distribute income and assets within each fund to individual child (i.e., cannot give money from one trust to the beneficiary of the other trust).
Trust taxed at higher level because earnings greater.	Trust taxed at lower level as earnings less.

21-Year Rule

The Income Tax Act prevents settlors from sheltering taxable property gains in trusts indefinitely. Just as property is deemed to be sold on the creation of the trust (***first deemed disposition date***), the Act also deems that capital property be deemed disposed of every 21 years from the date of the contribution to the trust and taxed accordingly. Therefore, if you create a testamentary trust and you die on January 3, 2003, all the property assets of your trust still existing in 2024 will be 'deemed' sold. Even if your trustees keep the property in the trust, they must pay capital gains taxes on the assets as if they were sold. Knowing this, in advance, will help you, as best you can, plan to have sufficient other assets in the trust to cover those costs every 21 years.

Furthermore, according to the Accumulation Rule, income from the trust must also be distributed after 21 years as it cannot be accumulated for more than 21 years.

Assets and Funds That Can Go Into An Inter Vivos Trust

Trusts are very flexible and, therefore, can include any of the following assets.

1. Cash and cash pledges including contributions by family members, the beneficiary herself, grandparents and extended family, friends, neighbours, colleagues and interested people.

2. Insurance policy benefits.

3. Real property.

4. Investments such as stocks and bonds.

5. Limited partnership interests and private businesses.

6. Collectibles such as coin and stamp collections, antiques, art.

Testamentary trusts may have all of these assets plus the residue of a person's estate or a portion of that residue as described in the will.

Taxation of Income Earned and Capital Property

Trusts are usually treated as 'individuals' by the Income Tax Act. Since the assets are permanently transferred into the trust (except in revocable trusts), the settlor, trustee and beneficiaries are not taxed on the earnings. All earnings are attributed to the trust. However, if part or all of that income is paid or payable to the beneficiary, it may be deducted in calculating the taxable income of the trust and taxed as income to the beneficiary (probably at a lower tax rate).

Note:

- The inclusion rate of capital gains was reduced to 50% from the previous 66 and 75%, effective October 18, 2000, if the anticipated legislation is enacted.

- Spousal testamentary trust or dispositions of an estate to a spouse will result in **no** tax until the death of the surviving spouse which results in a deferral of tax that may be attractive within certain families.

Taxation is usually different for inter vivos and testamentary trusts. Income retained in an inter vivos trust is taxed at the top personal marginal rate but special rules may enable income to be taxed in the hands of beneficiaries. Taxation within a testamentary trust is on the same scale as personal income tax. The taxation rate will change depending on the total taxable income within the trust. For example, in the case of parents in a high tax bracket, rather than the first parent to die leaving all their investments and assets to the remaining spouse who is already taxed at the highest taxation rate, the first-deceased parent can create a testamentary trust naming the remaining spouse the trustee (thereby, keeping control of the funds within the family) and the children as beneficiaries. They would save several thousand dollars in taxes per year on a trust with $100,000 in it earning interest at 10%. Those savings would compound over the life of the trust with large income increases for the beneficiary.

Following the death of a parent, if a testamentary trust is established, the Income Tax Act deems that the deceased disposed of any capital on October 18, 2000. The testamentary trust acquires such assets at the same value. Therefore, if the family cottage is put into a testamentary trust for a young child, then it is the value of the cottage upon death that is taxed. For example: the parents bought a cottage 30 years ago for $20,000. When they die and the property is put into the trust, it is valued at $150,000. The capital gain is $130,000 ($150,000 - $20,000). The Income Tax Act uses only 75% of the capital gains to calculate taxes owed. In this case, then, the capital gains are assessed as $97,500 ($130,00 x 75%). The parents are taxed at the highest taxation rate of 50%, therefore, the estate must pay $48,750 ($97,500 x 50%) in income tax. Good estate planning can minimize this tax burden and provide the maximum contribution to the trust (e.g., an insurance policy, other investments to cover the tax). Note: if the trust later sells the property for $200,000, the capital gains would be assessed based on the difference between the sale price and the deemed value at the time the trust was established ($200,000 - $150,000 = $50,000 capital gains). After October 18, 2000, the inclusion of capital gains is reduced from 75% to 50% of the capital gains.

When a testamentary trust distributes real property to a beneficiary, the property is taxed according to the increased market value of the property at the time when it became part of the trust. For example, the parents bequest their income-producing property in the trust for their daughter and it was valued at $150,000 on the death of the parents when it was contributed to the trust. The trust holds onto the rental property for 10 years, until the daughter is deemed mature enough to have the home in her own name. The value of the rental property, for income tax purposes, is still $150,000 although the true market value of the property may have increased to $350,000. If the daughter sells the property, it will be taxed on $200,000 increased value less deductions.

Tax considerations play an important role in estate planning. Get competent tax advice to minimize your taxes so you will have more income and capital for your beneficiaries. There are numerous techniques to minimize and/or avoid taxes besides trusts. These can include gifting, estate freezing, charitable donations and others to discuss with the appropriate professionals.

Trustees

Trustees are as important to choose as an executor of your will. This person, or persons, should ideally be able to:

- Live up to a standard of honesty, due diligence and care which represents the legal standard of what a reasonable and prudent person would do in carrying out their duties, (professional trustees are held to a higher standard of knowledge and care).

- Make unbiased decisions in the best interest of the beneficiary consistent with the settlor's wishes.

- Understand the settlor's morals and principles (useful in making investment decisions).

- Understand why the trust was established. Professional trustees, in particular, should understand whether you want that trustee to maximize the size of the trust for the benefit of the final beneficiary as opposed to spending the money for the benefit of the person for whom you set up the trust.

- Understand investment alternatives and make sound investments without incurring unnecessary risks.
- Understand basic financial management (e.g., be able to maintain, record and balance accounts, understand compound interest).
- When necessary, hire agents or advisors to help in managing, investing and distributing income from the trust while recognizing that final decisions belong to the trustee.
- Live near the beneficiaries in the case of a disabled beneficiary.
- Commit the time and energy necessary to manage the trust, invest the assets, and distribute the principle and/or income while also spending time with the beneficiary as needed.
- Use an **even hand** in making investment decisions to, as much as possible, benefit all beneficiaries equally, unless stated otherwise in the trust agreement.
- Live a long time to fulfil their duties (i.e., do not pick an elderly person to be trustee of a trust expected to last 30 years).

- Understand and apply the provincial rules and regulations of their respective Trustee's Acts.

- Act in ways that are not profitable to the trustee and detrimental to the beneficiary.

- Avoid conflicts of interests between themselves and the beneficiaries.

Trustees can be family members or friends. They can also be professionals in private practice (e.g., financial advisors, accountants, lawyers) or at a bank or trust company. Alternates should be provided for in the event the Trustee dies or becomes unable or unwilling to continue to act.

Trust Fees

There are several ways that fees are charged for creation and maintenance of a trust:

1. When getting professional advice from a financial planner, lawyer and/or tax accountant, you will be charged their hourly rate or a package rate. This depends solely on the complexity of the trust you wish to establish, the time incurred, the degree of professional expertise, and the size and nature of the assets involved.

2. To create a trust:

    a) A domestic inter vivos trust may cost between \$600-\$2,000 if it is relatively simple. More complicated trusts will cost more.

    b) A domestic testamentary trust in a will is less expensive since the legal fees are already incurred when creating your will. Start up costs can be several hundred dollars to over $1,000 depending on the complexity of the trust.

c) International trusts for living or testamentary trusts depend on which country the trust is created in and how complex the trust. Although there may be tax advantages to creating a trust outside of Canada, you should ask whether the fees will cost more than the tax savings.

3. To maintain a trust: Fees will vary considerably depending on the circumstances, such as the size and nature of the assets, degree of skill required, the performance of the trust's investments, etc. Some provincial legislation sets out the fee range payable to a trustee(s). In other jurisdictions, it is best to shop around to get the best service for the most reasonable fees. The annual care and management fee is usually based on the capital assets of a trust, its annual results and complexity and ranges from 0.25% up to 0.6% per year. The fee is generally divided between the revenue receipts and revenue disbursements. A further fee may be charged on the capital receipts and disbursements. There may also be an annual fee for preparing the trust's income tax return. When there is more than one trustee, the fee may be split evenly or unevenly depending on the allocation of responsibilities, time incurred and expertise. One or more of the trustees may act voluntarily, without a fee.

4. Closing a trust: Usually, when a trust is closed and the assets are dispersed to the capital beneficiaries (those named to receive the remaining assets in the trust), a fee of between 1-2.5% of the assets distributed is charged by the trustee, again, depending on the size, complexity and time spent.

To understand fees, Sandra Foster writes[2]:

In general, assets of less than $100,000 would not be large enough to offset a minimum fee for the services of a professional trustee, and this cost may be discouraging. Questions to ask the trustee about fees:

Are there annual fees: (check correct answer)	**Yes**	**No**
For preparing the income tax return?		
For managing the assets, based on the value of the assets?		
For the services of the trustee?		
Based on the income earned by the trust?		
Based on the money paid out of the trust each year?		
For distributing assets to the beneficiaries?		

If 'yes', ask to see the fee schedule and for an estimate of the costs that would be charged. **Tip**: Trustee fees can be negotiated, especially if the assets are of significant value.

Once you have such an estimate, subtract it from the expected return on investment of your trust. Is there enough income earned:

---

[2] Sandra Foster. (1996). *You can't take it with you: The common-sense guide to estate planning for Canadians.* Toronto: John Wiley & Sons. Pages 168-169. Reproduced with permission.

1. To pay all the fees to both your chosen family trustees plus any professional trustees they may hire?

2. To cover necessary taxes?

3. To pay for services and needs of the beneficiary(ies)?

If yes, than a trust may be the right vehicle for you. If no, check with your lawyer and financial advisor to see if there are other alternatives more suitable for your situation.

So, Are Trusts for You?

After a brief explanation of trusts, do they apply to your situation? Can they provide some degree of financial independence for your loved one? Are they an effective estate planning tool for you?

For families with a disabled or dependent child or adult, trusts are a method of long-term financial and estate planning that are underused in Canada. With the basic understanding of the options in this chapter, you should be able to talk with a financial planner, lawyer and/or tax accountant to understand what are your best options and whether or not one or more trusts may benefit your loved one.

Chapter 4
Present and Future Needs

Last Will and Testament

This book is not a summary of preparing wills but Appendix C may help you with the basics. As well, the resources listed at the end of the book may lead you to useful resources beyond your own lawyer.

Less than half of Canadians have a will. People without valid wills will have their estate divided according to provincial laws (different in each province) with almost certainty that your assets will not be divided to the persons you prefer, at the time you desire or in the way you would choose. **You must have a will if you want to ensure the care and relative financial security of your loved ones and dependents in a tax advantageous way.**

There is no perfect will, however. You are never really finished making a will. You cannot wait for perfection. Draw up a will now with the best information you have. You can always improve on it over time but for now, if you die suddenly, the disbursement of your estate will be much closer to your wishes than if you leave it up to the legislatures and courts to decide.

As you get new information about what will make your will better, you should have a codicil to your will or a new will drawn up. Neither a codicil nor a new will is very expensive especially if it can save valuable assets and time later on.

Beneficiaries under insurance policies, jointly held assets, RRSPs, and inter vivos trusts receive their money or assets outside of probate and are available for almost immediate use by the beneficiary (except infants and minors). Alternatively, if the beneficiary of an insurance policy or RRSP is the estate, the proceeds will be subject to probate and will pass through the will or testamentary trust. There are advantages and disadvantages to consider with many options available.

Powers of Attorney

Powers of attorney are documents that tell others who you want to speak on your behalf when you cannot, or do not want to, speak for yourself.

There are two main types of legal powers of attorney documents that a person signs to delegate legal decision making to one or two people of their choice. The first gives one or more persons financial and property decision-making power from the time the document is signed until the document is revoked by the person. The second gives all health-care related decisions to the person names as power of attorney when the person becomes incapable of deciding for themselves. It may be advisable to separate the two types of documents so that one person is not responsible for all decisions and not in a conflict of interest (e.g., save money for the estate or spend it on extended homecare costs). However, it may also be helpful to have the same person or persons (e.g., a spouse, trusted child or friend) named under both powers of attorney to speed up decision-making and cut down on conflicts.

In the case of a power of attorney for financial and property matters, a person chooses one or more persons to act on their behalf because they are no longer able to do so themselves. Someone may choose to do this when they are legally competent to act on their own behalf but cannot physically get to the appointments, make the telephone calls, or keep up with the high technology that is becoming increasingly more common (e.g., telebanking, ATM machines, Internet banking).

The power of attorney for financial and property matters can begin immediately upon signing the document or only come into effect when the person can no longer competently act on their own behalf. The power of attorney may be subject to specific instructions and restrictions. Alternate attorneys should be provided in case the person(s) first named dies before they can fulfil their role or if they become unable or unwilling to act.

Assets and Liabilities

To determine what your loved one may need for short and long-term finances, you must do a complete assessment of your own financial situation and that of your loved one. The forms in the Appendix G may help with this assessment if your advisor does not provide you with their own forms.

Once you have a sense of the likely annual and long-term expenses you would like your trust's income to cover you can do the following math. For example, let us assume that your loved one needs about $40,000.00 in living expenses beyond what is available through government disability payments and other income they receive. Many fund managers suggest that a 7% return on investment is a reasonable average. Therefore to generate an average of $40,000 per year you would need a trust of about $572,000 (40,000 divided by .07). The sale of a family home, a life insurance policy or two, RRSP savings and contributions of family and friends could make up a large portion of this amount. The magic of compound interest would increase the principle of the fund if the beneficiary did not need all the income generated each year.

This is most probable when younger adult children may require less support and have fewer expenses than when they become older and have increased financial needs.

Chapter 5
Beginning, Maintaining and Closing a Trust

Banks, trust companies, credit unions, lawyers and investment firms provide in-trust accounts. For example, a lawyer uses an 'in-trust' account at her bank to hold money used in transferring ownership of a home or property. Legally, the lawyer cannot access the funds for her own use although the account is in her name. Once the sale is finalized, the buyer's money held in the trust account is given to the seller. This is not the same as a trust fund.

A trust fund must be opened by a legal document, usually prepared by a lawyer. This can either be an inter vivos trust (when the person or people creating the trust are alive) or a testamentary trust (through a person's Last Will and Testament). With this formal trust deed, the trustees can open up a bank account through which they can pay bills, invest funds, pay taxes, etc. The trust is a 'legal person' under tax law and, therefore, the trust can hold, sell, invest, loan, and borrow as any other person.

Trusts are powerful tools and require you to spend as much time shopping for the correct trust format with the correct institution to meet your needs as you would shopping for the right family car (i.e., look at safety, longevity, service, performance, liabilities, and competition).

Once you have reviewed the information in this book about trusts, speak to the various professionals who have a specific expertise in trusts, most particularly discretionary trusts if you have a financially dependent loved one receiving government benefits. The example in the Appendix D of a testamentary trust may be helpful. The financial planner, accountant, tax advisor and lawyer will then walk you through the various investment options for your trustees to consider upon opening the trust and the types of fees required to open, maintain and, finally, close the trust. The appropriate professional should be able to give you an idea of how much income can be predictably earned with various investment strategies minus the fees to earn those incomes. This will give you a sense of how much disposable income the trustees will have to meet your child's needs.

A detailed list of trustee responsibilities to maintain the trust is described in the Appendix F.

Remember that your trustees, carefully selected, will still not make all the decisions that you might make under similar circumstances. You may have given them absolute discretion to do what they think best under the circumstances to prevent a decrease in government benefits or you have given them reasonable discretion in other types of trusts. Trusts will not guarantee a perfect financial situation for your son or daughter but the trust will provide sufficient guidelines to help minimize mistakes.

Once a trust has fulfilled its purpose (this can take months or decades depending on what you have created) the trust must be closed. Again, there will be fees attached to this process that you should be aware of to ensure that the trustees will save adequate funds in the trust to cover these costs. See Chapter 3 for specific questions to ask about trustee fees.

Chapter 6
Non-Financial Considerations

Although Part 2 of this book is primarily about **financial security** for dependent loved ones, the emphasis in real life must be on the person's inter-dependence **emotionally**, **physically**, **spiritually**, and **socially** with those around them. A rich person isolated from their family and community is worse off than a poorer person surrounded by a loving family, friends and a community that recognizes and accepts their gifts.

To put financial considerations in their proper context, one must look at a person's life holistically. What is it that they have to offer others? What is it that they need from others? Financial planners, estate planners and ever-increasingly popular life-planning counsellors suggest we look at all aspects of a person's life.

Appendix E is a detailed template of a life plan looking at a person's personal data. The following life plan was designed by Janet Klees and is presented here with her kind permission. Her life plan is a planning tool used to describe a vision for a person's life. Klees works with families who have adult children with developmental disabilities. As she writes: "I'm more comfortable doing each plan from scratch for the individual, but in reality the following 'format' is one way to include the key areas I want to include in each plan I help to prepare. My fear right now is that this format will make people think about writing an Individual Program Plan as was required by the Ontario government in the 1990s. Those plans were exercises in highlighting a person's disabilities and weaknesses. Our life plans are about helping the individual, their families, friends and communities **highlight the person's abilities and gifts**. I've only included the boxes in order to suggest the kinds of things that might be written in that area. Another format might be to use cloud designs rather than boxes to show their flexibility and adaptability more strongly. Each family could also eliminate the boxes entirely and put the information together in other creative ways. One family could write a life plan by simply writing out the person's life story with their hopes and dreams for the future; another could use photos or drawings to illustrate the points, etc."

A Vision for Life

It is important -- even essential -- to hold before us a positive, well-articulated vision of a good life for each person. This vision can provide us with direction in times of confusion when one must choose between many choices. The vision can provide us with ideas and possibilities in times of trouble, with a way of setting priorities in times of scarce resources, and with hope. A clear vision that is communicated among and shared by the people who care for the person most is our best hope for a good life for them, now and in the future.

We want this person's life to contain the same things that all of us would include to describe a good and meaningful life for ourselves:

- A place to call home.

- Safety and security in one's home and wherever they go in their community and wider abroad.

- Connections to family, friends, and a wide range of acquaintances - people who value them for their own unique combination of character, gifts, talents, and strengths.

- A sense of belonging -- people who value their presence and miss the person when they are not present.

- A place or places to give, participate, and contribute in meaningful ways that are recognized, appreciated and welcomed.

- Spending their days in personally fulfilling ways.

- Continual opportunities to grow and expectations that they will grow and learn throughout their lifetime.

- Respect of those with whom they come into contact.

- The opportunity to make good, well-supported choices and to be involved with governing the direction of their life.

- Good health as a result of living a healthy life style.

- A few close and committed relationships with family members and friends, and an ever-widening circle of those committed to be with them on their life's journey.

- A way to communicate with at least a small circle of people who understand them well and care to listen to the deeper messages within their actions and responses to situations.

- Hope for the future.

- The opportunity to work on a few of life's dreams at any given time.

- A satisfying spiritual life.

We are committed to finding ways to achieve or sustain the vision of this life for and with this person. The plan is that this person's life will look like the following:

Home

Issues of safety and security

A place of peace

Welcome, and place that others want to be

Where this is – either a precise address, or a neighbourhood, or a type of dwelling with whom this might be shared

Family

Ongoing relationships, not dependent upon parents

Respect and belonging

Connections throughout time

Holding many family roles -- daughter, aunt, niece and cousin

Friends and Other Relationships

Personal committed relationships

Ongoing nature of developing new relationships and deepening others

Mutual respect, shared interests

Opportunities to be a friend, as well as having friends

How Person Spends Their Days

Typical household management routines

Holding a range of valued social roles connected to work, volunteering, pursuing interests, etc., and the importance of safeguarding these

Following the rhythms and routines that are typical and valued and followed by age and gender peers in the community

Work - part time, full time, ideal number of hours and when during the week

Opportunities to contribute to their community

Health

Healthy lifestyle choices - food, exercise, avoiding intoxicants, regular check ups

Specific choices for any conditions or health concerns

Recreation, Leisure and Hobbies

Importance of maintaining a balance in life

As opportunity to grow and learn

As a place to meet people and make friends

As place and time to participate and contribute to one's community

The arts as opportunities in some way for each person to grow at home as well as outside interests

Lifelong Growing and Learning

Courses, interest groups, formal pursuit of knowledge

Travel, and other ways of learning through experience

Opportunities to make real choices, be supported in more complex decision-making

Participating in the other choices which govern her life

Growing ways of effectively communicating choices

Positive interpretations of choices that have been made

Support circles as a way of offering and safeguarding choice

Engaging and understanding civic duties

Spiritual

Church and other formal religious

Tradition, ritual and other private and personal ways of living a life of meaning

Dreams

Possible identification of hopes and dreams that now seem remote or even impossible

Other (e.g., financial needs)

Annual income need of $______________

Special funding needs for (e.g., own home in future, transportation, travel, communication tools) of $________

Other

An Example: Naomi's Life Plan

Naomi Terry is a young woman living with her parents, Emma and John, in Scarborough, Ontario. They have all agreed to allow us to reprint Naomi's Life Plan as an example of how such a plan was actually drafted. It is important to individualize the plan and include the person's name often to highlight we are discussing a person's life, not a framework or theory of how to 'treat' or 'manage' people's lives. Janet Klees took her vision framework and used it to help Naomi and her family draft out this plan. Naomi has an active support circle that has reviewed this draft and uses it as a basis to acknowledge Naomi's many gifts and talents. From this overall plan comes daily and weekly plans and activities discussed and implemented to find the best ways for Naomi to live fully and joyfully. The overall plan remains consistent while daily and weekly planning is adapted to meet changing needs and opportunities.

Vision

It is important -- even essential -- to hold before us a positive, well-articulated vision of a good life for Naomi. This vision can provide us direction in times of confusion, solace in times of trouble, priorities in times of scarce resources, and hope at all times. A clear vision that is communicated to, and shared by, the most important people in Naomi's life is our best hope for a good life for her -- whether or not her parents are present.

We want Naomi's life to include the same things that all of us would include to describe a good and meaningful life:

- A place that Naomi calls home.

- Safety and security in her home and wherever she goes in her community and wider abroad.

- Connections to family, friends, and a wide range of acquaintances -- people who value her for her own unique combination of character, gifts, talents, and strengths.

- Support, as required, offered by a range of caring, knowledgeable family members, relatives, neighbours, friends, co-workers, and paid support assistants.

- A sense of belonging -- people who value her presence and miss her when she is not present.

- A place, or places, to give, participate and contribute in meaningful ways.

- Spending her days in personally fulfilling ways.

- Continual opportunities and expectations that she will grow and learn.

- Respect of those with whom she comes into contact.

- Good health as a result of living a healthy life style.

- A few close and committed relationships with family members and friends, and an ever-widening circle of those committed to be with her in her life's journey.

- A satisfying spiritual life.

We are committed to finding ways to achieve or sustain the vision of this life for and with Naomi. As this vision becomes reality, Naomi's life will begin to include the elements described below.

The most significant parts of our vision for Naomi centre around her desire to remain in her present family home and the vital importance of the loving circle of family members, friends and support persons in her life. Naomi indicates often that she wants to remain at home, even when her parents are no longer able to be with her. Her greatest fear is that she might be returned to a group home and that she might find herself alone when we are no longer here. Our vision, therefore, describes a future where:

- Naomi will live in her family home with her parents for many years to come. The family home has been recently renovated to provide two complete, and (potentially) separate living arrangements. Naomi's parents will gradually live more and more fully within their own quarters, as Naomi grows in her ability and comfort to live more and more independently (with a variety of formal and informal support) within her part of her home.

- Naomi will never have to worry about having to leave or move away from her home, unless she clearly and explicitly decides this within the support of her circle over time. It is extremely important that Naomi be free to remain in her home for as long as she wishes. When her parents are unable to provide direct support, Naomi will begin to share her home with one or more persons – people that she has come to know over time and whose combinations of gifts and talents will match well with her own. Her parents' quarters will be available for this companion (individual, couple, young family) who will then provide security, continuity, and some support to Naomi in exchange for a room and board stipend.

- Naomi's home will never resemble a group home. A group home comes about from two interconnected situations: a congregation of two or more vulnerable people with needs to be met; and a set schedule of routines, procedures, and safety requirements that cannot be individualized to one person without infringing upon the needs of the other. Support in her home will always be centred on Naomi, and routines and procedures will adapt to both her need for predictability and for accommodation at a given moment. These conditions will be almost impossible to meet when support people are also trying to meet the needs of another individual with disabilities.

- Naomi will use the funds of the Options program to provide support assistants who will help her to develop and maintain the necessary life skills to allow her to be as involved in the day-to-day management of her home life as possible. The support assistants will always be woven into the support circle of family members and friends who have been a part of Naomi's life over time.

- Naomi's home will be a place of security and sanctuary to Naomi always. It will be a place of welcome and hospitality to the many friends and relatives who are a part of Naomi's life. Family, friends and visitors will enjoy spending time in Naomi's home.

- Naomi's sister and brother and their families will always be actively involved in her life. When time and distance (Mississauga and Florida) take them away as daily contacts, they will remain involved in planning, advocating, and supporting with the rest of Naomi's circle. They may also be available to move in with Naomi if the need arose.

- Naomi will be fully supported by a wide range of caring, knowledgeable family members, relatives, friends, neighbours, co-workers, and paid support assistants. These people will be sensitive, creative and thoughtful in meeting her changing support requirements and other needs. They will do so in ways that ensure that Naomi maintains maximum control and input over the direction of her life.

- Whether the supports for Naomi are provided by family, friends, a live-in companion, or paid support (and probably a combination), Naomi will always be surrounded by a caring and supportive network. This network or circle will need support to ensure their ability to advocate for Naomi. This will involve someone who knows Naomi well and loves her dearly ensuring, on an almost daily basis, that she is being treated kindly and in her best interests. It is not adequate to have someone who does not know her, check in on Naomi and her support on a set day once a week, because if the wrong kind of support were present, Naomi's vulnerability would prevent her from being able to speak up for herself.

- Naomi will be involved in a network of relationships, from casual acquaintances and co-workers, to welcoming neighbours and close family and friends. A significant number of these will be personal, committed relationships with individuals who are interested in ensuring that Naomi continue to lead a satisfying life and who will take a role in making sure this happens, if necessary.

- Naomi will hold a number of strong, positive roles in both her home and neighbourhood, and will be surrounded by a number of people who understand and recognize the importance of safeguarding and promoting such roles for Naomi at all times.

- Naomi will be engaged in some sort of regular part-time work (possibly a small business venture) from which she derives at least some income and a great deal of pleasure. This work will be enhancing to her image, will offer her challenges and opportunities, will be work which is highly valued by the community at large, and will make use of Naomi's particular gifts, skills and interests.

- Naomi will spend a part of each day and each week meaningfully engaged in managing her household (shopping, banking, cleaning, cooking, laundry, etc.) in ways which allow her to be involved in her home and life in significant ways.

- Naomi will be involved in a rich variety of recreation and leisure opportunities both at home and in the wider community. Many of these will change over time to suit her growing and changing interests, but at least a few will reflect important, enduring leisure pursuits that Naomi chooses to follow.

- Naomi's dietary, sensory integration and medical needs will be taken into consideration in a holistic way by all those who know and support her. Meeting these requirements will be naturally integrated into appropriate parts of Naomi's days and weeks as necessary.

- It will be expected that Naomi will always have the potential and interest in personal growth and development throughout her life. She will continually be offered positive, achievable opportunities to learn new skills, and grow and develop in many areas.

- Naomi will make ever-widening choices in life -- some on her own initiative, and some with varying amount of support from those who know her best. People who are in Naomi's life will be creative in finding ways to make sure that she is participating in the choices which govern her life.

- Naomi will have a range of positive, effective ways to communicate her choices, thoughts, concerns and joys. She will be surrounded by people who are able to understand her well.

- Naomi will gather together with her support circle of family and friends regularly in order to celebrate, to plan, to coordinate, to dream and to support one another in hard times.

- Naomi will have opportunities to grow and give, in heart and spirit, in a spiritual community that has meaning for her and offers her peace and satisfaction.

A Brief Appraisal
Where Are We Now in Regards to the Vision?

Home

Naomi is living at home - where she wants to be. Challenges for the future include:

- How to ensure that this continues even after her parents are no longer able to be there?

- How to make sure that her home always feels like home, and never feels like a group home to Naomi?

Relationships

Naomi currently enjoys a wide range of relationships -- her sister, Gwendolyn, is back in town and so is her new brother-in-law John Edward. Her wide, extended family (especially aunts and uncles) are a very important part of her life. She has relationships with her pastor, Father William, and with members of her church. She has a large and active circle with over 20 members. The relationships with these members vary, and in some instances are deepening.

Challenges for the future:

- Provide opportunities for meaningful, committed personal relationships with extended family members (cousins, aunts, uncles).
- Work on mutual friendships (and more) with her age peers.

Support

Naomi is currently well supported -- by family, friends, neighbours, and paid supporters. Challenges:

- Finding, guiding, and keeping paid supporters working at ensuring that an inner circle of people really understand what good support for Naomi means.

Valued Roles...A Place in Community

Naomi holds a number of positive and valued social roles: pianist, artist-craftsperson, photographer, volunteer, church member, and more. Challenges:

- To maintain and deepen current work and leisure roles
- To ensure that the positive roles are safeguarded so that in times of changing schedules to meet other needs, the opportunities to fulfil these important roles are not lost (e.g., if Naomi is feeling stressed by her week, the piano lesson, the community exercise class, and her work take priority over other obligations).

We are grateful to Naomi and her family for sharing this life plan. Her life stories are inspirational.

Chapter 7
Family Story (The Sequel)

Susan and Johan Vivas (from Chapter 2) took a multi-pronged approach to securing the financial future of their children, Jessie and Mark. Jessie is now 22 and continues to live at home. She works at a different store in the mall and has increased her volunteer work at the provincial park. Mark is in his first year of university studying business. Susan and Johan:

1. Have spent time preparing a thorough life-plan for their financially-dependent child, Jessie, including defining a vision, examining long-term housing options, work possibilities and her financial needs. They also examined how Mark's short-term education needs (he is now 19) and long-term financial needs can be met.

2. Helped develop formal and informal support circles around Jessie so that there would always be a network of support nearby when the parents were no longer able to provide that support themselves. They found that Jessie's circles were also very supportive of Mark at this age and would be there for him should his parents die suddenly in the near future.

3. Discussed their plans and the likely financial resources remaining after their deaths with their children with the result that Mark decided he wanted a smaller share of the parents' assets as he fully expected to have the financial means to take care of himself in the long term. This wish was accommodated by putting both children within one discretionary trust and leaving it up to the Trustees to determine how the funds should be divided between Jessie and Mark to accommodate changing circumstances in their lives in the decades ahead.

4. Worked with a lawyer to draft up a new will including provisions to establish a single discretionary trust for both children. As Mark is only 19, their present will has been written to provide for his short and medium term needs. In 10 years, they will review their will and revise it to recognize Mark's financial status at that time. It is likely that a larger portion of the family assets will go into the trust for Jessie. However, Mark's entitlement to his share of the family assets will continue to be provided for by making him the beneficiary of his parents' RRSPs (outside of the probate process).

5. Secured the commitment of three people to serve as primary trustees (family member and two friends), along with the trust company and support circles, in securing the financial stability of their children.

6. Will review every two years their plans and wills to ensure that they still meet the specific needs and circumstances of their children.

On going through this process, the parents said, *"at times we felt overwhelmed. How could we begin? Who would even want to be involved? Will people need to know all our private thoughts? How can you put on paper what you want?"*

To answers these questions they met with other parents and heard what they thought and what they were doing. "*We took one step at a time and realized that planning is continuous and always changing. Inviting a network of support around our children provided us with a feeling of relief— other people, who know our children, will be there for them when we are not.*"

Like most parents in this situation, Susan and Johan had a natural tendency to procrastinate about the larger concern of financial security for their children when their day-to-day needs already seem overwhelming. They suggest that *"people call a lawyer who has had experience with writing wills that include discretionary trusts. Taking this step to write or revise your will is actually an easy step. The lawyer does most of the work. When you are ready, you can add to or change parts of the will as you learn more about the kinds of things that might be helpful. Keep proceeding slowly. Find someone who will encourage you to plan. This person might be at your local Association for Community Living or another family you know. It is difficult with our busy lives, but you feel more secure knowing that you are putting things into place."*

Susan and Johan have given us permission to reproduce Susan's Last Will and Testament (all the names have been changed). Her document is the same as Johan's Will. (See Appendix D: Sample Discretionary Trust Created by a Last Will and Testament). This sample may help you in preparing your own will and asking your lawyer about relevant legislation in your province. However, do not copy this will out for yourself. This wills works for the Vivas family and their particular circumstances. Your will must be specific to you and your circumstances and be drawn up by a knowledgeable lawyer in your own province.

Part 3:

Endowment Funds

Chapter 8
Deohaeko Support Network (The Beginning)

The Deohaeko Support Network is a group of 7 families with adult children who have disabilities. They began meeting in each of their homes over meals to discuss alternative living arrangements for their children other than the typical group home or institutional options more commonly available in their communities. Over time, they decided to create their own charitable organization with the purpose of (a) organizing the day-to-day support planning (formal and informal) for their daughters and sons, and (b) securing funds from the federal and provincial governments to build a co-op housing project. They were one of the last groups in Ontario to secure those kinds of funds and they built a 105-unit housing co-op apartment building in Pickering, Ontario in 1994, called the Rougemount Co-Operative.

They have successfully secured some annualised support dollars for their daughters and sons from their provincial government and they commissioned a book (1996) about their hard-fought successes, *We Come Bearing Gifts*, by Janet Klees, to help other families in similar circumstances. Deohaeko families have come up with a unique way of sharing support dollars among all families, based on varying individual requirements each year. They pool the government funds and decide, as a group, which portion each family will get to meet the projected support needs of each daughter and son. The families then use those dollars to hire support staff as needed. Supporters are generally not shared between families.

At various times throughout the year, a family may request a few more dollars to meet unexpected needs, or they may return unused dollars to the common pot to be used by another individual. Through this give-and-take approach, Deohaeko has a good idea of how many support dollars may be required in the future.

Aside from planning and helping to meet the day-to-day needs of their children, the group turned their attention, in 1998, to the financial future of their children. At that time, the parents were (a) providing countless hours in direct support for their children on principle but also because they only had about 50% of the annual funding they needed for support, (b) constantly lobbying to maintain their current funding, and (c) trying to discover ways to ensure the financial security of their children in the future after the parents are no longer physically able to provide direct support or after the parents die. They estimated that they would need an endowment fund of approximately $5,000,000 to provide annual support dollars of about $300,000 to $350,000.

The families recognized that they must rely on two pre-conditions to prepare for the long-term security of their children:

1. Financial security that would supplement the ongoing funds their children were receiving through government benefits but never to the point where paid support represented the total care provided (i.e., informal support and care were still of primary importance).

2. A supportive network of committed people who would be there voluntarily for each son and daughter through support circles of family, friends, neighbours, work colleagues and, of course, members of each other's support circles.

In researching alternative ways of ensuring their children's financial stability, they were immensely frustrated by the lack of information available to families in similar circumstances. Banks, trust companies, credit unions and investment firms were either ill equipped or ill informed to advise them. To get even the simplest banking or investment information seemed an exercise in frustration. Using their experience in building the co-op apartment building as a guidepost, they decided to do the research and share their knowledge with other families through the production of this book.

Deohaeko families understand that the endowment is just addressing direct support funding for their children. Each family is also looking at setting up trust funds for their son or daughter to assist them with other aspects of daily living or unexpected support needs.

Chapter 13 provides an update on their efforts.

Chapter 9
What Are Endowment Funds and Are They for Us?

Endowment funds are simply a financial product available through banks, trust companies, credit unions, community foundations and investment firms to allow an organization to contribute cash and other assets into a fund as principle. The principle earns interest and part or all of that interest can be given out while the principle is usually left untouched. The endowment fund is completely separate from operational funds.

Endowment funds appeal to organizations that struggle with yearly fund-raising to have enough funds to continue their mission. Creating an endowment fund for a specific program or for the operations of an organization may minimize or avoid the amount of bake sales, annual fund-raising drives and special events that an organization must participate in each year. These fund raising efforts eat up their pool of volunteers and staff who could be using that time to actually fulfil the mission of the organization. An organization must consider, however, if it has enough time and energy to raise an endowment fund without taking too many resources away from fund-raising that is needed to secure enough money for this and next year's operations.

Endowment funds are different than the reserve funds that every organization should have when it occasionally has more revenues than expenses. Reserve funds have both the principal and the interest available for any use decided upon by the Board of Directors. Endowment funds usually have only the income (interest on the principle) available to the Board.

Endowment funds make long-term planning possible. They provide a predictable amount of interest income each year.

Before determining if an endowment fund is right for you, it is useful to look at the difference between not-for-profit and charitable organizations. The differences between them may affect your decision to create a fund or not.

Not-For-Profit and Charitable Organizations

The not-for-profit and charitable organizations of Canada have almost 12 million members, and represents about 12% of Canada's Gross Domestic Product since almost nine percent of the labour force is involved. The organizations we think most of when we think of charities are the hospitals, universities, school boards, churches and disease-specific groups that try to find cures. There are nearly 180,000 not-for-profit and charitable organizations in Canada and we donate over a billion hours of our time to these culture and heritage, professional, recreational, spiritual, trade, volunteer associations, and advocacy organizations.

About 100,000 organizations are considered not-for-profit. The other 80,000 are considered both not-for-profit and charitable organizations. They both must be incorporated and operate under the leadership of a board of directors with no intent to earn a profit. They do not pay income tax but must file special returns and financial statements to Canada Customs and Revenue Agency (formerly Revenue Canada). Not-for-profit organizations do pay taxes on investment income while registered charities do not. Not-for-profit organizations have less accountability to government since they cannot issue income tax receipts to donors and, therefore, can provide non-profit products and services with less administrative and bureaucratic record keeping. For example, where a charity may have to do a means test to see if a client is 'poor' enough to receive their charitable service, a not-for-profit organization does not.

Registered charities are able to offer tax credits, through income tax receipts, to their donors. There are basically three types of charities: (1) charitable organizations that carry on specific charitable tasks, (2) public foundations that raise funds and distribute them to one or more other registered charities (e.g., a hospital's foundation that raises funds for specific programs within the hospital, community foundations), and (3) private foundations set up by families and public community foundations to distribute grants to other registered charities.

Charitable status in Canada is based on an antiquated view of what charity is as defined by the 1601 English law called the *Statute of Elizabeth* and updated in 1891 by the House of Lords. The latter version categorized charity under four categories, which are still used in Canada today: the relief of poverty; advancement of education; advancement of religion; and a restrictive category of purposes seen as beneficial to the community.

Charities must fulfil their mission through the appropriate use of its resources. They must spend 80% of the amount of funds raised in the previous year for which they issued tax receipts (called the *Disbursement Quota*. This helps to ensure that most of their funds are used for charitable purposes, that expenses are kept to a reasonable level and that excessive funds are not accumulated. Exceptions to this rule include bequests from wills, gifts from a registered charity, and donors that require the charity to hold the gift for at least 10 years (e.g., money put into an endowment fund).

An extensive, two-year study of the entire volunteer sector was completed by Ed Broadbent's cross-country panel with the resulting report, *Panel on Accountability and Governance* recommending an expansion of our definition of what constitutes 'charity' with increased accountability through an impartial, arms-length government agency to investigate and deal with fraud and misuse of charitable funds, similar to what is done in Great Britain. The recommendations have yet to result in changes to the registration and investigation of charities.

Pros and Cons of Establishing an Endowment Fund

Endowment funds for not-for-profit and charitable organizations can be an effective way to ensure the long-term financial security of your work. As with all financial decisions, however, there are pros and cons to establishing such a fund.

Pros

1. The main attraction for small not-for-profit and charitable organizations to create an endowment fund is financial security or even independence. At some point, an endowment fund might have enough accumulated principle and interest to provide an organization with annual operational funding without further fund-raising. This is particularly possible for small organizations that need less than $500,000 in annual funding.

2. An endowment fund can be sub-divided into several 'named' funds so that families, organizations and foundations could contribute a portion of the fund in their name or in honour of someone. Minimum amounts may be set to minimize the administrative costs of

tracking many small funds. However, minimum standards might be waved for children and adults with low incomes who have an interest in donating to a fund as a beginning step to life-long contributions to not-for-profit and charitable organizations. (See Chapter 1 for further information on 'named funds'.)

Cons

1. The main drawback for small not-for-profit and charitable organizations in creating a fund is that money being raised for the fund might be better spent on fulfilling your mission. For example, if your organization is struggling to have enough operational dollars to help people who are poor meet their daily needs, then putting aside valuable resources to be used in 10 years from now may be inconsistent with your mission to relieve poverty.

2. Donors may restrict the use of their donation within an endowment fund that may make it more difficult to use the income from the fund for sudden changes in the organization's mission based on current needs. For example, a donor may contribute to a fund with the restriction that it be used for research. At some future date, however, the Board may decide that pressing current needs will require a diminished amount of research work.

   Organizations should accept restricted donations if: (a) the restrictions fit within the organization's mission, (b) they are non-discriminatory, and (c) include a power-to-vary clauses that permits the Board to reallocate the income from the donation for pressing current needs or if the original restriction of the donation no longer applies (e.g., a donation made to maintain a new support program but that program is later paid for by other, ongoing operational funds).

3. Many banks and trust companies will only open up an endowment fund if an organization has a minimum of $500,000. Some banks will not open up an endowment fund unless it is larger than $10,000,000.

4. If you find an institution that will house your fund, you must still determine if the income you can earn outweighs the financial and time costs to create, maintain, manage and fund raise for your endowment fund. The costs may outweigh the benefits for smaller not-for-profit or charitable groups.

Chapter 10
Present and Future Needs

If endowments are a useful tool for your organization, you must begin with an analysis of your present and future financial needs. Using your mission statement, strategic plan (if any), program descriptions, past 3 years accounting statements and future cost projections:

What are your present and projected assets and liabilities?

What are your present and projected yearly financial needs? *(Divide this figure by the approximate annual interest rate expected to get the approximate size of the endowment fund you will need. For example, if your annual operational budget is about $100,000 and the expected rate of return on the fund is 5%, after expenses, your will need about a $2,000,000 endowment.)*

Are your present needs being met consistently? If so, how are present needs being met?

How will an endowment fund campaign affect present fundraising, if at all?

Check with similarly sized organizations that have done this process successfully. Most organizations are keen to help similar, non-competitive organizations achieve success modifying their own strategies.

Get the help of experts in this field through books, videos, library resources, and interviews with endowment fund experts and sales representatives. Collect the information in ways that make it more likely that you will make the right decisions. Compare apples with apples by creating forms that help you compare the advantages and disadvantages of each institution's products. (See Appendix A: Comparing Trust or Endowment Funds form for an example.)

In Deohaeko's research, community foundations provided the most economical method of creating and maintaining an endowment fund for small charitable groups. Community foundations are charities established across Canada and the U.S. through which families and smaller charities can establish an endowment fund. By pooling these endowments into one large fund (like a mutual fund), community foundations are able to provide expert management and investment skills at reduced fees. They also provide the administrative structure to send out income tax receipts, file income tax forms, send statements to their contributors as well as raise funds for their own operating costs. Lastly, community foundation provide the mechanism to disburse the interest income from the endowment funds either to pre-determined charities as chosen by the fund creators and contributors or through an application process similar to the United Ways where groups apply for undeclared funds.

Not-for-profit groups would have to partner themselves with a registered charity to create a fund and have income from the community foundation fund channelled through the charity because community foundations only distribute income from their fund to registered charities. **(Community foundations are explained more fully in the next chapter.)**

Chapter 11
Beginning, Maintaining and Closing an Endowment Fund

If you have chosen to begin an endowment fund and you have an idea, from the previous chapter, of how much principle you need to raise, you can begin the paper work!

An endowment fund is like an organization's long-term savings account. It is a way of developing your financial asset rather than just another fund-raising tool. It is your way of securing and providing future services to your fund's recipients.

Beginning Steps

1. Discuss the possibilities of an endowment fund at the Board.

2. Assign staff and/or volunteers to do some preliminary research into creating a fund for your organization by checking with community foundations (described later in this chapter), banks, and investment groups. Present this research to the board.

3. The Board of Directors must make a firm commitment to the development of an endowment fund. Creating a fund will take up their time as well as other resources within the organization. The Board may select a working committee of members, staff and outside volunteers to help with the following tasks.

4. The Board recruits or assigns Board members and Advisory Members with a special expertise or interest in endowment funds to help them with decision-making.

5. The Board, or its committee, must determine if any of its operational dollars from government, public or private foundations, or major donors are at risk if they establish an endowment fund. For example, if endowment-fund dollars are used to provide support to people labelled poor or disabled, will those benefiting from your services have any of their government or disability pensions or payments 'clawed back' or withdrawn?

6. The Board needs a policy statement outlining the purpose of the fund, how funds will be distributed and when, and what should happen if the original purpose of the fund is fulfilled (i.e., how to close the fund). Like an organization's mission statement, this step can be the most time consuming. However, once a policy statement is in place, the rest of the steps have the necessary direction to make the process move more smoothly.

   The policy should include:

   a) The overall and specific purposes of the endowment fund.

   b) The name of the fund.

   c) The type of fund the Board approves (i.e., mixed portfolio or only fixed income).

   d) Financial objectives of the fund meaning that the investments appreciate over time to cover the revenue needs of the fund, its administrative and investment expenses and a value equal or greater than the Consumer Price Index (CPI) to cover inflationary costs. Although this return will not happen every year because of the market and economy's ups and downs, it should be expected over the long term.

e) Spending rules including that the principal shall not be touched for at least 10 years, except when income is insufficient to meet the 4.5% disbursement rule (more information on this later in this chapter). All other interests and dividends can be given to the charity or its specific programs, reinvested in the endowment fund and/or put into the organization's reserve fund to be used as needed. If the Board wants to be able to use the principle in the endowment after 10 years, it should clearly identify circumstances when that would be appropriate.

f) How the fund will be structured (e.g., a general endowment with specific named endowments) and how units of the fund will be determined and valued, and when donations can be made to the fund.

g) How the fund will be managed within the charity (i.e., by the Board or by the finance or special committee reporting to the board) including what decisions can be made by whom:

   i. Investment and management policies, and their revisions.

   ii. Choosing and changing investment managers as required, upon evaluation of fund returns.

   iii. How the fund will be invested (i.e., % invested in equities, fixed income and cash equivalents).

   iv. How income is given out.

   v. Minimum amounts for named endowments within the fund, if any.

h) How contributions can be made including a sample of an agreement between the donor and the organization.

i) How individual funds and/or the entire fund can be closed and where the proceeds of the fund(s) would go.

7. The Board might also consider a policy statement that all, or a major portion of, unexpected gifts to the organization be put into the endowment fund. Such a policy encourages a quick decision about what to do with unexpected gifts rather than the common back-and-forth arguing between members, staff and/or volunteers of what to do with such gifts.

8. The Board must decide whether it is advantageous to create a separate foundation to create and manage the endowment. Such a foundation, with its separate charitable registration, can ensure that staff/volunteers within the present organization concentrate on your organization's mission while staff/volunteers of the foundation can concentrate on the endowment's creation, development and ultimate funding of your organization. Such a separate body can provide donors with an added sense of comfort and accountability and sense of longevity.

   Such a separate foundation, however, has major drawbacks for small charities since it requires a separate board, separate registration (and all those costs), separate meetings and minutes, separate records and the potential of conflict between the two boards in how the money should be used.

   More on this later in this chapter.

9. The Board should develop an action plan for the following steps including who will do what, by when with sufficient follow-up procedures to ensure the work is done appropriately.

10. The Board needs to research and choose the advisors it will use to create a fund. These advisors may include a combination of: a financial planner, a lawyer with expertise in financial products, and an accountant familiar with the tax implications of such a fund.

11. The Board needs to research and choose the institution where you will house your fund. If you are a registered charity you may choose a community foundation to pool your fund with those of other organizations and individuals. (See Part 4 of the Appendices for a complete list of community foundations nearest to you.)

12. If you have sufficient funds, open up your fund using the documentation required by the institution.

13. If you do not have sufficient funds or after you have opened up an endowment fund, prepare your marketing material including brochures, pledge/donor cards, donor agreement forms, etc. The fundamental tenet of fundraising is: "*It is easier to ask if you first give*", so give prospective donors the necessary information they need on planned giving, benefits to donations, mission of your organization, etc. before you try to secure their donation.

14. Identify potential donors from your present donor list including those who have included you in their will, follow up with past donors, and identify new donors through personal and professional contacts and through referrals. Also become known to the estate and financial planners in your various communities as the better

informed they are, the more likely they will recommend your work to others. Provide a free 'wills clinic' to encourage people to prepare a will and, perhaps, include your organization in it. Prepare a script to use in approaching new donors to help them understand the purpose of your fund. Endowment funds are built through long-term relationships with current and potential donors. It will take time. Review this process each year, set new targets, revise procedures as needed and re-energize your group to ensure the long-term success of your fund.

15. Annually, do an evaluation of the above process, your assets, future planning cycle and changes necessary to achieve your goal.

Community Foundations

Community foundations are geographically based foundations that pool named funds of families, community organizations and charities into one endowment that helps fund local community charities. There are 97 community foundation across Canada with total assets of $1.2 billion in 2000.

Capital is owned by the foundation and held in perpetuity. The foundation is run by a Board of Directors as a registered charitable organization which is tax-exempt, incorporated, organizationally autonomous, and cannot be controlled directly or indirectly by any level of government, or by corporations, associations, members or individuals.

The foundation provides donors with a professionally managed endowment fund and donors can have their own portion of the fund named after themselves or in honour of someone. The foundation does all the administrative work including some or all of the following: giving out income tax receipts to other donors who wish to contribute to your fund, prepare audits and tax returnes as required, and issue reports. One usually needs $10,000 to open an endowment but methods are available to help people and individuals start with less.

There are different forms of endowments within the one Community Foundation Fund. Each community foundation across Canada defines them slightly differently but generally they are:

1. ***Designated funds*** are created by a person to support a particular charitable agency or organization (i.e., the Smith family creates an endowment to support a charity that assists local families with children who have disabilities).

2. ***Donor advised funds*** enable donors to participate in the distribution of income from their fund but the final decision is left to the Board of Directors of the foundation.

3. ***Agency endowed funds*** enable charitable organizations to create their own endowment fund but have the Community Foundation do all the administrative work and the donation is not an asset on your financial statement. As the creator of the fund, you designate how the income from the fund is disbursed -- usually to yourselves as the designated charity.

4. ***General and thematic dispursements funds*** allows donors to contribute to the general endowment fund or to a specific field of interest undertaken by the foundation such as: arts and culture, childrens' groups, education or environment. Donors can specify the type of cause they wish to contribute to (e.g., services to seniors) or leave it

up to foundation to choose which charity will receive the income. In the latter case, the Board of Directors, similar to the United Way, asks for grant proposals and decides which local charities will receive funds. Some community foundations have chosen specific areas of concentration for such grants (e.g., local arts and recreations, social service agencies).

5. The foundation may have opened up an endowment of their own within the general endowment fund in the expectation that donors will want to assist the foundation in its work and, thereby, reduce adminsitrative costs charged to each fund.

Since the fund is a pooled endowment, the fund is usually large which allows for a more diversified portfolio of assets and, therefore, better returns with lower administrative costs. There are no legal fees in setting up a fund with the foundation.

A 'variance' clause directs the foundation's board to find "the nearest similar purpose" should the intended purpose of your fund become irrelevant (e.g., a fund to sponsor research in breast cancer becomes irrelevant as soon as a cure is found) or the designated charity stops operations. This clause ensures donor confidence that their long-term investment in your work will continue in perpetuity.

Check your local telephone book for the community foundation nearest to you or check the list in Part 4 of the Appendices. These foundations are geographically based within communities although some have a wider reach (e.g., The Vancouver Community Foundation provides grants province wide in British Columbia).

By opening an endowment with a community foundation, a charity may contribute to it regularly, raise funds specifically for the endowment and build the fund to a point where the interest income can fulfil its goals (i.e., either for the cost of a specific program or for the operational expenses of the charity). In Deohaeko's case, the families have determined that a fund would need about $5,000,000 to provide the families with annual operating dollars of about $350,000.

Creating a Separate Foundation

Should charities set up separate foundation to take over their fundraising? Such a foundation, with its separate charitable registration, can ensure that staff/volunteers within the present organization concentrate on your organization's mission while staff/volunteers of the foundation can concentrate on the endowment's creation, development and ultimate funding of your organization. Such a separate body can provide donors with an added sense of comfort and accountability and sense of longevity.

Such a separate foundation, however, has major drawbacks for small charities since it requires a separate board, separate registration (and all those costs), separate meetings and minutes, separate records and the potential of conflict between the two boards in how the money should be used.

Pros

1. If your charity is asset rich, (e.g., owns property, investments, a large endowment fund) and is at risk of being sued by clients, then a separate foundation can be an advantage in that it can hold the property and lease it to the charity to prevent creditors access to these assets. For example, if a small charity provides services to clients

in a building it owns and a client sues the charity for staff negligence, then all the charity's assets are at risk. However, if the endowment fund, building and other assets are held by a separate foundation, those assets are safe.

2. A separate foundation permits a charity to have two separate boards of directors with different skill sets. The fundraising and money management skills required by a foundation board are different than the policy and program decisions made by a charity board. The boards can be smaller, more manageable and more focused on their own skills sets. Some members would be on both boards. The foundation's direction comes from the charity's board and all the funds raised by the foundation go to the charity.

3. A separate foundation can benefit charities that receive a lot of government funding. Since the charity's assets are separate from donations to the foundation, government funding to the charity (up till now) cannot be cut because of assets held by the foundation.

Cons

1. Separate foundations require a separate board (recruited and trained), separate registration and bylaws (and all those costs), separate meetings and minutes, and separate records.

2. Initially, a separate foundation's board will be highly compatible with the charity's parent board. However, over time, there is likelihood that the foundation's board (responsible to both donors and the charity) will suggest or require the charity to change its focus and programs to meet donor demand. The foundation may begin to

require the charity to submit funding requests for specific programs rather than for general operations as programs are easier to raise funds for than general expenses. The charity's board may be more finely attuned to the needs of their clients than the foundation's board even with a cross over of several board members on both boards. As each organization is legally separate, the opportunity for conflict increases over time and the foundation may come to a point where it changes its mandate to allow it to fund other charities consistent with donor wishes. This has happened in the case of hospital foundations where the hospital has been merged, acquired or closed but the foundation continues.

3. A separate foundation's priority is raising funds, especially for the long term. This priority may be in conflict with the parent charity's mandate to provide short-term relief of poverty or short-term care to clients in need.

4. Conflicts are possible in promoting the charity and foundation's work through the media and other promotional avenues. Who speaks for the work of the charity? Who speaks for the clients served? Who speaks for the donors? The answers may seem obvious that fundraising questions be answered by the foundation, but in real life, distinctions blur especially when reporters are in a hurry and don't have time to ask some questions of the charity and some of the foundation.

5. Separate foundations have more stringent disbursement rules than a charitable organization. While regular charities must disburse 80% of receipted donations from the year before, foundations must additionally dispense with 4.5% of the value of the investment assets each year. As well, 100% of donations made by charities to private foundations must be spent in the following year. For

example, if a charity received $50,000 last year it must use $40,000 of that this year. If a separate foundation received that $50,000 last year and added it to its $100,000 of assets, it would have to use $40,000 of that this year (80% of $50,000) + $6,750 (4.5% of $150,000). However, if that $50,000 came from another charity, the foundation would have to spend all of it + 4.5% of its assets.

6. In 1995-96, The Office of the Public Trustee in Ontario made it very difficult to establish foundations whose principal object is to raise funds.

7. New accounting standards may require accountants to disclose the foundation's assets and income on the financial statement of the parent charity, thereby, preventing a parent charity from keeping endowment funds held by the foundation from government view.

To minimize some of the negative aspects of separate foundations, small charities must consult with both legal and tax experts with specific experience in this field. The charities should also talk with small charities who have similar programs to their own and which have separate foundations to discuss the pros and cons. After these discussions, and with samples of by-laws from foundations set up for small charities, a charity can determine if a separate foundation makes sense in their specific circumstance. If a separate foundation is established, its by-laws should be reviewed every few years to ensure that both the foundation and parent charity continue to work toward the same goals.

Maintaining

The endowment fund may be divided into one or more separate endowments depending on your circumstances. Rather than creating different funds for different purposes, it is best to create one fund (better purchasing power). Administratively, this is easier than keeping track of various separate sub-funds. To track the individual worth within a single fund of the separate endowments is similar to how mutual funds assign units to each individual member of the fund. See chapter 1 for an example.

You will require a semi-annual or annual review of your fund's performance and ongoing communication with the people you have entrusted to manage your fund. You will need to maintain or revise the authority structure within your Board or Committees to ensure that you truly are on top of the fund's performance, and any irregularities or difficulties that occur. It is important that your Board be aware of any changes in the laws and regulations regarding these funds and taxes.

Disbursement Rules and Endowments

If a charity receives a gift or bequest with the donor's written instructions to hold the donations for at least 10 years, the 80% disbursement rule will not apply. If the charity receives an unrestricted bequest and decides to invest the funds in its endowment, it will also not be subject to the 80% rule. However, in both cases, the charity will be required to distribute 4.5% of its capital every year, which will normally come out of the income, earned on the investment.

Investing the Fund

Boards should choose investment managers that reflect their style and long-term needs. Typically, an endowment fund should have a total return, less expenses, that permits sufficient income to meet both the 4.5% distribution requirement of endowment funds as set by the Canada Custom and Revenue Agency and its own current revenue needs.

Agreements with Donors

When a donor makes a large contribution to your endowment fund through an outright gift or irrevocable deferred gift (e.g., such as a life insurance policy), the donor and organization should have a signed agreement that will:

1. Identify and gratefully acknowledge the contribution and wishes of the donor (including, perhaps, a bit of biographical information about the donor for future members of the organization to better understand the donor, the heirs and the circumstances of the gift).

2. Clearly state the purpose and administration of the endowment fund.

3. Contain legal language that satisfies Canada Customs and Revenue Agency's 10-year distribution quota rule.

4. Allow donors to pledge future or ongoing gifts (e.g., monthly) for a determined or undetermined period.

5. Provide clauses that permit the organization to change restrictions if the original intent of the donor can no longer be met or if the organization's mission changes to

meet current needs unforeseen at the time of the donation.

6. Provide an opportunity to amend the agreement at any time with the signed consent of both the donor and organization.

7. Explain what will happen with the donation should the fund be closed.

If an agreement cannot be mutually signed, a letter or a person's will signed by the donor and containing the necessary instructions can be enough.

Reporting Back to Donors

Donors, especially ones to endowment funds, deserve regular (semi-annual to annual) reports of how the fund is doing and how the income is being spent to meet the purposes of the fund. When significant events or information is available, that should be sent to donors as well. Whenever possible, write a personal note to the donor to help them recognize how valuable you feel they are to your work and mission.

Donor Recognition

Many donors would prefer to remain anonymous and that should be respected although a regular personal note to them will always be welcome. Others prefer some public acknowledgement of their efforts on your behalf. This can be through a listing in your annual report, description in your newsletter, special announcements or special events recognizing regular or endowment donors, acknowledgement in publications produced by the group and other creative ways.

Closing

The process of closing an endowment fund must be included in the design of the fund. Most small not-for-profit or charitable organizations will not continue forever. Either their mission has been met (e.g., another program takes over the needs within a community) or the volunteer commitment to continue the organization is no longer there. Whatever the reasons, endowments must have a clearly defined closing policy so donors will be aware of what happens to their contributions should the organization close the fund. For many such endowments, the simplest solution would be to have the fund either converted into the fund of another charity or not-for-profit with similar goals or to have the principle and income dispersed to a variety of other similarly minded organizations. The Board of Directors at the time of closing the fund should have sufficient discretionary powers to make the best decision possible consistent with the overall goals of the fund and its contributors and to report on their decision to their donors.

Chapter 12
Non-Financial Considerations

It is easy to get caught up in the excitement of creating an endowment fund that will answer all of your financial needs sometime in the future. What is less exciting, yet more important, is to look at the non-financial considerations of your organization and whether the endowment fund will foster or hinder those considerations.

This process is best done from the perspective of the people you serve and the people from whom you hope to get donations. They can best evaluate if your organization should exist in the long-term. No matter the desire of the founders or present leaders of organizations, there are many small organizations that have either outlived their usefulness and are only there to provide staff with a job or they are duplicating the work of others.

Answer the following questions, to ensure that an endowment fund is really what you need now or in the future. The answers will tell you, as objectively as possible, whether the non-financial considerations will work with, or against, an endowment fund campaign.

- What is your purpose as an organization? Are you achieving your purpose now and/or do you foresee yourself achieving your purpose in the future? Are you remaining true to your mission or are you moving from one activity to another just to get government or foundation funds? Does everyone in your organization understand and work consistently to meet your purpose? Can everyone articulate what you do and why you do it? If there is a lack of clarity of what you do and why, then funders and the people you serve may well hesitate to provide you long-term donations for an endowment fund.

- How long do you expect your organization to stay active (many organizations have a shorter life span by design or by circumstance)? For example, an organization established to relieve poverty among single parents living in an urban centre probably has a long-term need given our collective human failure to end poverty. However, another organization's short-term purpose may be to provide poverty relief in a small community undergoing dramatic changes due to a short-term economic downturn. Only long-term organizations should consider endowment funds.

- Will an endowment fund campaign take away more financial and human resources than you can afford? If your organization is struggling to meet its program demands and fulfil its obligations to its members, then you should not start an endowment fund campaign. If your small organization is starting and wants a secure funding base before offering services and support, then an endowment fund may be appropriate, although hard to raise funds for as it has no track record. If you have a successful program running with some financial stability but are unsure of whether that funding will continue in the years ahead, you may well consider an endowment fund.

Once you have answered these questions as honestly and completely as possible with leaders within your organization, you will have an idea of whether an endowment fund fits in with the crucial non-financial considerations.

Chapter 13
Deohaeko Support Network (The Sequel)

Throughout 1999 and 2000 the 7 families that make up Deohaeko Support Network hired, on contract, a part-time staff person to research what their alternatives were and what type of agreement the families would have to reach to create a fund. Deb Thivierge helped them decide how income from the fund would be used, what would happen as families left and joined Deohaeko, and more. They used several weekend retreats to thoughtfully analyze their best options. Combined with the research done on this book and the information they received from several lawyers, family groups and financial institutions, they determined that:

1. Their target of a $5,000,000 endowment was correct.

2. A community foundation was the most economical and well-managed institution in which to place their fund.

At the start of this process, however, the families established an interim investment account to house the money they had being raising for the fund until they could decide where to put their endowment fund. They had not yet heard of community foundations and had assumed that a bank or trust company was the likely place for their endowment fund. Although several banks and an investment firm provided bits of information, the advice was slow in coming and incomplete. Through sheer frustration, the families looked at other options.

Before a specific institution could be picked to hold their endowment fund, the families had other decisions to make. To open an endowment fund required an agreement among the 7 families of how the fund's money would be used, what would happen if a family left Deohaeko, what needed to happen if new families joined Deohaeko and how they would participate in the fund, and more. The questions seemed endless with few simple answers.

Through a creative game developed by Deb Thivierge and Janet Klees (Deohaeko's co-ordinator), the families were given a host of scenarios during one of their retreats. Each scenario was based on a letter from an anonymous donor or board member triggering a situation requiring a board response. Some of the scenarios represented situations the families had already considered while others were new. For example, a major concern for the board was what would happen if a family left Deohaeko? The game involved the families having limited discussion time and then voting (using beans) with varying time lines (7 to 20 minutes) and the results being recorded for later discussion. By getting this straw vote after a quick discussion it was possible to get a sense of where the group was on each issue and then allocating the necessary time to discuss each point. Sometimes there was almost unanimity. As so often happens, it is easy to have long discussions before people recognize that they are, in fact, agreeing with each other. On other issues there was a very mixed response requiring a more detailed discussion of alternatives.

Scenarios included:

- How the money could, and could not, be used.
- Whether donors could specify what their contributions could be used for.
- Whether donors could have named funds within the general endowment fund.

- How families could help raise funds.
- How new families would benefit from the fund.

The results of these discussions led to a draft agreement among the families that they reviewed at their November 2001 retreat. On the issue of what would happen if a family and the son or daughter left Deohaeko, for example, it was agreed that they would not be entitled to any income from the fund. In effect, they agreed that the endowment fund belonged to Deohaeko and not to the families who helped set it up.

After revising and agreeing to the new draft, the families sought the advice of two lawyers familiar with these issues for a last review. The revised agreement (see Appendix L) was approved and negotiations with the Community Foundation of Durham Region began to discuss opening their endowment fund by the end of the Spring, 2002.

The families agreed that other families considering a similar process of creating an endowment fund would need: patience, energy, sufficient information, time (should not be rushed) and a willingness to go beyond typical fundraising.

As one parent said: *Patience, patience, patience. Even people you think should have knowledge don't always have the knowledge you need. From a personal point, I wish we'd started this 20 years ago when ability, energy and knowledge would be at a higher point than they are now. A large lottery win would be marvelous.*

Another parent suggests that families *join a group of like-minded people to share your stories. It would be difficult to do on our own without the support of others who care and feel as you do. It can be rewarding but be aware of all the work involved.*

The process took Deohaeko several years of collecting information, meetings, ongoing discussions between families and negotiating with potential fund holders. It can get frustrating trying to make the 'right' decisions, however, the slow process is necessary to cover all aspects of an agreement and successful endowment fund. Be patient. The results are worthwhile if properly planned.

One parent summarized their process this way: *Deciding to create an endowment fund was the easy part--developing the agreement was a good process. Our group has worked well together and have made many decisions in many areas. Discovering how to create an endowment, where to get good information, who could help a small group such as ours, who would walk through this maze with us, was a horrendous task. Fund raising is ongoing and our small group even got good at it. It needs to happen. It takes time, energy and good ideas.*

The financial future and security for our children was extremely important. Preparing our wills with a proper discretionary trust and designation was necessary. These allow our children to have extras in their life and safeguards that they will not live in poverty. A very important piece is to ensure dollars are there to provide sufficient funds to have good supporters. This financial piece needs to be well planned. Hopefully government continues their role but we as families also need to have alternate plans. Planning our endowment for Deohaeko is a wise move.

Part 4

Making It Work For You

Chapter 14
Creative Fund Raising

Does one fund raise for their child's trust fund? Why not? Although much of the following information relates to charities raising funds, there are certainly opportunities for families, friends and neighbours to raise funds for a specific person's trust fund. Although a trust cannot give income tax receipts for most of these contributions to a fund, there are ways to contribute that may reduce an individual's income tax. Check with your financial advisor/accountant before asking for contributions. Some of the following methods, including the planned giving of insurance policies, stocks and bonds, contributions through wills, etc. can be adapted for a trust fund. Some of the donation projects may also fit well in increasing the assets within a trust fund. Do not be limited by these ideas but rather encouraged to develop your own.

According to Stephen C. Nill, Editor of the *American Philanthropy Review*, 50% of the parents of baby boomers will be gone in the next 15 years. These parents own 75% of Canada's personal wealth. As much as $4 trillion will be released in Canada in the next 40 years with half by 2015. Creative fund raising provides strategies and methods to help this group, plus others, maximize their giving (charitable or otherwise) with optimum tax benefits.

This chapter does not examine standard fund raising. Therefore, we will not look at how to organize special events (e.g., bake sales, fashion shows, art sales, auctions). Nor will we look at participating in a local lottery or gambling ventures such as BINGO games, Las Vegas tickets, or raffles (funds raised through such ventures in Ontario, for example, cannot be used for endowments). Lastly, we will not cover direct mail, affinity credit cards (i.e., credit cards with your charity's name on them and you receive a small percentage of the charges made on the card), telephone or door-to-door solicitations or media events such as telethons. The library, bookstores, government and fund-raising organizations have many books and resources in these fields.

We will look at methods that have particular relevance to raising funds for trust and endowment funds. Since we are dealing with relatively small numbers (less than $5,000,000 in most cases) we will depend mostly on relationship-building methods that involve donors directly in the lives or projects involved.

Before we look at the specifics, it may help you to understand the concepts behind the Rule of 72.

About Interest on Your Investments: The Rule of 72

Compound interest is an invaluable tool to increase the value of your assets without having to work at it. If you invest your funds and do not remove any of the interest, the interest and principle grows every year. Depending on the rate of return on your investment (e.g., 7%, 10%) your money will double quite quickly. This is true whether you are creating a trust or an endowment fund using investments in GICs, money market bonds, stocks and bonds, income or other investments. Note that the example does not look at the tax implications (e.g., capital gains, income taxes), the costs of maintaining the investments (i.e., management and/or administration fees), the consequences of income generated on any of the person's income-tested benefits (e.g., government benefit payments), nor on the risks and returns on various instruments which are not fixed. The rule is designed only to give you the overall picture of how funds can multiply over time.

This rule is critical to understanding your investment options. Just mentioning the rule to a financial advisor will impress them with your basic understanding of investment basics.

The Rule of 72 tells you how long it takes to double your investment. It is simple. Take the interest rate you expect to earn on a particular investment and divide that number into 72. Whatever the answer is, will give you an estimate of how many years it will take for your money to double. For the above example, we assume you only invested one lump sum. In reality, you will probably continue to invest annually toward your fund but this will give you some sense of how long it will take without doing anything other than making one, initial investment.

Three conservative examples (i.e., not including the stocks that go up 40-200% in a year):

Investment at 5%	**Investment at 7%**	**Investment at 10%**
72/5 = about 14.4 years	72/7 = about 10.2 years	72/10 = about 7 years
Take the next step. Assume you have $50,000 in RRSPs or other investments **that you do not touch for the next 20 years**. In the three examples above, you would have:		
Doubled after 14.5 years and another $40,000 in the next 5.5 years = $140,000	Doubled twice in 20 years = about $200,000	Doubled almost three times = about $400,000

Remember, in the examples above, it was assumed that you began with only one initial investment and never added anything to the principal yourself. For most of us who put something aside each year, the above examples would be even more impressive as compound interest plus your own contributions over the years will dramatically increase your assets after 20 years.

In cases where trusts or endowment funds are established with one major investment (e.g., sale of the family home, pay out of an insurance policy, large donation) you could double your fund in about 10 years on average with a 7% interest return each year.

There are two main sources of creative fund raising today:

1. Planned giving
2. Special donation projects

The keys to success in fundraising include:

1. Fulfilling and communicating your mission with emphasis on solving long-term problems rather than alleviating short-term crisis.
2. Understanding the current tax system and benefits to donors (it changes regularly). People want to make a difference in the world while also reducing what they perceive as over-taxation of their assets.
3. Focusing on developing long-term relationships with donors, to the degree that donors want, so they see their donations creating real-life benefits to others.

First Steps

After looking at all the fund-raising options outlined in this chapter, you need to start with a gathering of people interested in the financial stability of your loved one or not-for-profit/charity (usually around a good pot-luck supper!). I recommend food be involved in some way as the best community organizations have always centred themselves around the communal meal. Gather around the table all the people most intimately connected with the project. If you have too many people, divide them into groups around several tables. You ask them to bring their personal and work address books with them. Then you ask them to creatively think and write down all the people within their address books who might be even faintly interested in your fund. Ask them to include the spouses, children, parents and friends of those people within their address book. For example, your Aunt Judith's husband may have a connection at the local steel mill or gas station or your neighbour may belong to the local Rotary Club. Ask people to think beyond the norm and not to censor their selection at this point. This is only a draft list of potential contacts that they will keep (i.e., this list will not be copied and given out to anyone else).

Perhaps at another meeting, ask people to review the list of methods described below (feel free to make copies for everyone beforehand). Have people examine the list to narrow down the type of methods your group wants to use. For a person's Discretionary Trust, for example, you may begin with more planned giving alternatives such as asking family and friends to consider a bequest in their will to help reduce taxes on their estate.

Out of this discussion you will have narrowed the methods with which you will begin your fund raising. You also have the draft list of initial contacts. Beside the names on your list, write down which method you think will have the greatest likelihood of success. Keep in mind that your funds are probably going to be best served by initiating or continuing long-term relationships with those who will contribute and that you will not build up your fund to its target with only one visit to each person on the list. This will take time but the time is well spent both for financial reasons but also to build commitment within your family and your community to the purpose of your fund.

Secure an ***Advisory Committee*** to help you understand what is possible locally. Include trust and endowment fund officers or advisors, legal and tax advisors, a financial planner, people with previous experience in setting up a fund. Use this group (usually by telephone calls and only a few group meetings) to answer your questions that come up throughout this process.

Planned Giving

Planned giving is both a combination of methods to provide assets to a fund but also, in the case of charitable organizations, a way to minimize or reduce income taxes for donors. The benefits to donors will depend on their age, lifestyle, number of dependents and their specific needs and interests in contributing. Donors may give gifts while they are alive or through their wills after their deaths. Once made, most donations cannot be taken back.

Most of the following information applies to both not-for-profit and charitable organizations that want to set up endowment funds as well as families setting up trust funds. The key difference is that charities have the added benefit of providing donors with income tax receipts. Families and not-for-profit groups must rely solely on the good will of donors willing to contribute after-tax dollars, in most cases, although some contributions will reduce taxes as described in the chapter on trust funds.

Have your lawyer prepare different acceptance policies for different types of donations to your trust or endowment fund. For example, your fund may not be prepared to accept donations of real property like a cottage. If you will help donors create charitable remainder trusts (described later in this chapter), then you need a formal contract of agreement between the donor and the fund's administration. Such agreements give potential donors a clear idea of what is possible through their donation and what restrictions there might be with respect to trusts or donor-directed endowments.

Keep in mind, that governments change the rules on charitable donations regularly. Check with a tax accountant or lawyer to ensure that your plans are consistent with present laws and regulations.

The following are considered charitable gifts: cash, right to future payments such as life insurance, and gifts in kind such as stocks and real estate. NOT considered charitable gifts are time and services (e.g., a lawyer donating their legal work), used clothing or worn-out furnishings, and gifts from which you benefit (e.g., the meal and theatre portion of tickets sold by a charity -- therefore you get a receipt only for the gift portion).

Cash donations are still the most common form of contribution but this is changing. People can make one donation or may prefer to make ongoing contributions over months or years. The longer a person contributes regularly the more likely they are to be interested in some of the other methods listed below. They are also more likely to be interested in the long-term viability of your fund and the purpose of your fund. **Note:** some companies have a matching-gift programs that doubles an employee's contributions to a charity. Have your regular donors check their company's policy.

Another source of cash donations for endowment funds are gifts ***in memory,*** or ***in honour,*** of someone. Whether it be to honour someone's silver anniversary or in memory of a loved one who has died, such occasions can be a powerful opportunities to add substantially to an endowment.

For trust funds and not-for-profit organizations, there are no tax benefits to contributing to such funds. The benefit comes in knowing that a donor's contributions are extending their present good will into the long-term future success of your fund.

For charitable organizations, at present, a person can give up to 75% of their net income to charity and declare that on their income tax returns. There is an advantage to save your donation receipts (for up to five years after the donation) so they total more than $200 as the federal tax credit of 17% applies to the first $200 and then 29% above that.

Using present-day tax rules, here are the actual costs of donating $1,000 and $100,000 (e.g., from the sale of a home, insurance policy pay out, RRSP) to your charitable organization.

Total Donation[3]	$1000	$100,000
Federal Tax Savings First $200 x 17% Balance at 29%	 $34 $232	 $34 $28,942
Total federal tax credit	$266	$28,976
Provincial Tax Savings (48% of federal tax credit)	$128	$13,908
Total Tax Credit	$394	$42,884
After-Tax Cost of Donation	$606	$57,116

Therefore, when someone contributes $1,000 to a charity, they receive a tax credit of $394. The actual cost of their donation, then, is $606. If they contribute $100,000, the actual cost to them is $57,116.

Total tax credit is even greater when savings on federal surtaxes and provincial taxes are factored in.

Cash donations can come in various ways including: simple donation of cash and monthly donations based on automatic withdrawal from a donor's chequing account. Donors may choose monthly donations that are based on regular income received but not needed. For example, they may decide to donate any child tax credits, retirement income

---

[3] Heart and Stroke Foundation of Ontario's *Cash Gifts* fact sheet (August, 2000). Reprinted with permission.

from a RIF or government pension, or from a spousal benefit earned since the death of a spouse. This 'extra' income donation may provide the donor with a helpful income tax receipt while also allowing them to give more than they did before.

Pledge donation usually involves larger sums of money and involves either a pledge to donate an amount on a certain date (e.g., after a special event), for a charitable donation before February 28th of the next year to have their donation be considered for this year's Income Tax Form, or upon their death (through their will).

Publicly traded stocks, bonds, mutual funds can be donated with attractive tax benefits (except in Quebec) since changes were made in the 1997 federal budget. Rather than convert them to cash and donate the cash, people can save half the taxable portion of their capital gain on their income taxes for the appreciated value of their holdings by donating the holdings themselves to the charity. Before these changes, a person donating capital assets were seen as having 'disposed of their assets" for tax purposes with tax implications on the capital gains. If someone had earned $1,000 on their stocks, bonds or mutual funds and donated them to a charity, they would have to pay 75% of that as a tax on their gain. Now the taxation rate is only 37.5% on any capital gain and a donor can still qualify for a charitable tax credit based on the asset's fair market value. Your broker can transfer the stock electronically or you can endorse the share certificate to a charity. A tax receipt is issued for the shares' closing price on the day they are transferred electronically or the day the actual share is received by the charity.

An example:

Mary Taylor[4] bought $29,000 worth of shares in Company A, which is publicly traded. Today, those shares are worth $50,000 and she would like to donate them to a registered charity because she values their work and for tax purposes. Her combined federal and provincial tax rate is 46%. Let's look at two ways of donating this asset.

	Sell the stock & donate the proceeds	**Donate the stock directly to the charity**
1. Value of stock	$50,000	$50,000
2. Purchase price	$29,000	$29,000
3. Capital gain	$21,000	$21,000
4. Taxable gain	$14,000 (#3 x 66 2/3%)	$7,000 (#3 x 33 1/3%)
5. Tax credit for donation (#1 x 46%)	$23,000	$23,000
6. Tax on gain (#4 x 46%)	$6,440	$3,220
7. Net tax savings (#5-#6)	$16,560	$19,780

By donating the publicly traded stocks instead of selling the stock and donating the cash proceeds, Mary Taylor saves

---

[4] Heart and Stroke Foundation of Ontario's *Stocks* fact sheet. (August, 2000). Reprinted with permission.

more than $3,200 in taxes. By donating the appreciated stocks now, the asset is no longer in her estate that may have positive probate implications for her heirs.

Strip bonds are another financial tool that may benefit your endowment funds. Gary Ursell, of Richardson Greenshields, talked about their value to a meeting of the Greater Toronto Chapter of the National Society of Fund Raising Executives (1996).

Strip bonds are regular bonds issued or guaranteed by the government of Canada, a province or a foreign country. The interest coupons have been removed with the holder of 'strip' entitled to a single payment of a fixed amount (the face value) on the maturity date. No interest is paid in the interim. The purchase price (present value) is determined by discounting the amount of the payment to be received on the maturity date by the appropriate current interest rate or yield factor.

Possible benefits include:

1. Maturity date can be geared to almost any donor's income.

2. The only cost is the commission payable to the investment broker or advisor (e.g., $100 for a $25,000 bond). There are no trailer fees on maturity.

3. Strip bonds are traded on the commodities market where the field is very competitive.

4. Except if a life insurance policy holders dies suddenly, strip bonds are a better long-term gift to a charity because the maturity date and payment are known in advance and the donor may enjoy seeing the fruits of their donation while they are still alive.

5. Strip bonds, unlike life insurance policies, can be bought at any age, by smokers or non-smokers, regardless of the buyer's health.

Gift of insurance is a simple and effective way to make a substantial future contribution. You can either change the beneficiary of a present policy or buy a new policy specifically for this purpose. The annual premiums you pay every year on the policy qualify for a charitable receipt from the charity listed as beneficiary of the policy. Upon the donor's death, the insurance is paid directly and immediately to the charity. Insurance policies are outside of the donor's estate so the charity does not need to wait for the will to be dealt with or probated and the gift cannot be contested as in a will. Three options:

1. A person buys a new policy and makes the charity both the owner and the beneficiary. The donor receives a charitable tax receipt for full premium payment and the beneficiary can never be changed.

2. A person permanently changes the ownership and beneficiary on an existing policy (which is no longer financially necessary for its original purpose) to the charity. Donor receives a charitable tax receipt for the cash surrender value of the policy and any accumulated dividends within the policy.

3. A person changes beneficiary of the policy to the charity but leaves option open to change it again in the future. A charitable tax receipt cannot be issued for premium paid nor will the estate be issued a tax receipt.

Donating insurance is a cost effective way to make large contributions to funds. Consider, however, the cost of insurance if your health is not good, the tax advantages of contributing now (if you have the assets) rather than later through an insurance policy, and the need for an insurance policy to cover other needs or tax debts upon your death.

An example: John Jones[5], 43, would like to contribute $150,000 to his favourite charity but has no capital assets. He can buy a term-to-100 insurance policy on his own life that is guaranteed to be paid up in 10 years. He is a non-smoker and the policy costs him $3,000 per year, or $250 per month.

Total premium paid over 10 years	$30,000
Total amount of tax receipts over 10 years	$30,000
After-tax cost of policy (Assumes 8% federal surtax and provincial 48% tax rate)	$16,500

John Jones' monthly after-tax cost of the policy of $137.50 will lead to a $150,000 donation to his favourite charity.

Bequests of cash or other assets can be made through a will. Less than half of Canadians have a valid will, according to a recent Decima Research survey. Only 15% of those with a will had included a bequest to a charity and of those who did not make such a bequest, 44% said they would include a charity in a will, if they were asked. Yet bequests equal about 80% of planned gifts in the late 1990s. There is a large, untapped pool of income awaiting families and organizations willing to ask for some of it.

---

[5] Heart and Stroke Foundation of Ontario's *Life Insurance* fact sheet. (August 2000). Reprinted with permission.

It is always advisable to encourage potential donors to speak to you about their intention to make a bequest so you can provide specific wording for their will and special advice about how to make their gift even more helpful in reducing their tax load. In the year of death and the preceding year, the maximum donation that qualifies for a tax credit is 100% of net income, instead of the usual 75%. Keep in mind, that governments have increased this percentage over the years, but they can also decrease it in future budgets. Check with a tax accountant or lawyer.

Bequests can be paid out directly to the person or organization directly upon settling the estate or the bequest can be put into a trust fund with income going to an individual and, upon their death, the remaining assets going to a charity.

Bequests can be changed easily by changing a will so do not count on receiving the bequest as it may not happen. People are less likely to revoke a bequest if they are still involved with the family or not-for-profit/charity. Spend the necessary time and give the attention people deserve whether they end up fulfilling a bequest or not.

If making a charitable gift through a will, the person must write out the charity's full corporate name to prevent legal battles. For example, if 'making a gift to cancer', is the gift for the local, provincial or national cancer society in Canada or abroad? Is the gift for the Cancer Society or for a research organization with cancer in its title or to a hospital specializing in cancer treatment?

Different types of bequests:

1. A specific bequest is a gift of a specific property, cash amount, stock(s) or other assets.

2. A residual bequest gives the remaining amount in an estate, after all other aspects of the will are settled, including debts, taxes, administrative costs, to a specific person or organization.

3. A percentage bequest gives a specific percentage of the estate that goes to a person(s) or organization.

4. A contingent bequest comes into effect after other bequests cannot be met. For example, if the estate is supposed to pass to a person's remaining children but they have predeceased the person, the estate could go to a specific person or organization.

Bequests can go to organizations either as:

- ***Unrestricted***, i.e., "...to be used for the general purposes of ....(name of person or organization);"

- ***Restricted***, i.e., "to be used for the establishment or expansion of 'x' fund". With restricted assets, organizations should be notified, in advance, of the donor's intentions and the following clause (or something similar) put into their will regarding the assets use for a specific fund: "If, in the opinion of the Board of Directors/Trustees of 'x' fund, it should become impossible, inadvisable, or impractical to use this gift for the specified purpose(s), then the Board/Trustees may in their discretion use the gift to the best advantage of 'x' fund."

In the Heart and Stroke Foundation of Ontario literature they provide the following example[6]:

Joanne Woods left a $250,000 cash bequest to the Heart and Stroke Foundation. In the year of her death, Mrs. Woods reported taxable earnings of $149,000. Her executors can reduce her taxes payable to zero by claiming $130,000 of her total donation in her last tax return and the balance in the year preceding her death.

Bequest	$250,000
Income in year of death	$149,000
Charitable donation claimed on her last return	$130,000
Income in preceding year	$139,000
Charitable donation claimed for preceding year	$120,000
Tax saved for year of death (assumes 1998 tax rates)	$62,498
Tax saved for preceding year (assumes 1998 tax rates)	$57,859

Her total donation, after tax savings was $129,643.

Charitable remainder trust allows someone to transfer property during their lifetime to a trust and get an immediate tax benefit. The donor or another beneficiary receives income from the trust for life. Upon the beneficiary's death, the

[6] Heart and Stroke Foundation of Ontario's *Bequests* fact sheet. (August, 2000). Reprinted with permission.

remaining assets pass to the charity. This assumes the long-term viability of the charity. There are generally 4 steps to this process:

1. Donor irrevocably transfers ownership of some or all of their assets into a trust.

2. Donor establishes the terms of the trust.

3. Donor claims a tax credit.

4. The trust capital goes to the charity after the trust's beneficiary's death.

Using another Heart and Stroke Foundation of Ontario example[7]:

Howard Johnson, 68, establishes a charitable remainder trust by transferring stocks with a cost base of $450,000 and a fair market value of $500,000. He names himself as sole income beneficiary during his lifetime and the Foundation as beneficiary of the remainder of the trust upon his death.

These stocks had given him an annual dividend income of $10,000. Two months after the transfer, the trustee sells the stock and purchases bonds paying 7%. By giving this gift, Mr. Johnson more than triples his cash flow, reduces his taxes, and makes a significant future gift toward heart and stroke research and health promotion.

---

[7] Heart and Stroke Foundation of Ontario's *Charitable Remainder Trust.* (October, 1998).

1. Amount contributed to trust	$500,000
2. Donation receipt (based on 7% discount rate*)	$164,845
3. Capital gain recognized on transfer ($500,000-$450,000)	$50,000
4. Taxable gain (75% of $50,000)	$37,500
5. Tax on gain (assuming 50% tax rate)	$18,750
6. Tax credit (assuming a 50% combined credit of #2 x 50%)	$82,423
7. Net tax savings (#6 - #5)	$63,673
8. Capital gain taxed to trust when property sold	$0
9. Annual income before gift	$10,000
10. Annual income after gift	$35,000

Canada Customs and Revenue Agency has not given any guidelines for determining the discount rate. Usually a prime rate or a long-term bond yield is used. Sometimes the actual rate of return on the property transferred to the trust is used, assuming that the trust will retain the property.

Charitable gift annuity allows a person to deposit capital with a charity. In exchange, the donor receives an annuity -- a tax-advantaged, guaranteed income. The charity receives the remaining capital after the donor dies.

Canadians approaching or past retirement age are familiar with annuities. They deposit capital in return for monthly income. These income payments can be for a specified number of years or for life of one, or joint, annuitants. A charitable annuity has a similar structure but also has tax-free status, which can benefit donors. The benefits of a charitable gift annuity include:

1. Guaranteed regular income for life.
2. Freedom from investment concerns (this is handled by the fund managers).
3. Charitable donation receipt in year annuity is set up.
4. Monthly income payments combine capital and interest in such a way that there is little or no tax liability.
5. The asset is no longer in your estate, which may have positive probate implications for your heirs.

This method of creative fund raising is not advisable for people under 55 or for those who must provide a surviving spouse or dependents with income.

For example:

Janet Smith[8], who is 75 years old, makes a donation of $50,000 for a charitable annuity to her favourite charity. She will receive a guaranteed annual income of $3,000 for life. Her life expectancy, according to the annual mortality table prescribed by Revenue Canada, is a further 11.25 years.

---

[8] Heart and Stroke Foundation of Ontario's *Charitable Gift Annuity* fact sheet. (October, 1998).

1. Amount contributed	$50,000
2. Annual income	$3,000 (represents 6% of the capital contributed)
3. Life expectancy (1983 table[9])	11.25 years (table stipulated in 1997 to be used)
4. Total expected return (#2 x #3 = $3,000 x 11.25)	$33,750
5. Donation receipt (#1 - #4)	$16,250
6. Taxation of Income (a) Total expected income to donor annuitant (#2 x 9.68) 1971 table[10] (b) Amount taxable	 $29,040 (each payment consists entirely of capital return and table stipulated in 1997 to be used to calculate this sum) $0

[9] Revenue Canada stipulated in the 1997 Corrected Interpretation Bulletin IT-111R2 that the 1983 Individual Mortality Table is to be used for determining the amount of donation receipt (if any) for the life annuities and that the 1971 Individual Annuity Morality Table is to be used in calculating the capital/income portion of annuity payments).

[10] Same as footnote above.

If Mrs. Smith is in the 50% tax bracket, she would have to earn 12% on her $50,000 to generate the same after-tax income. Even if interest rate go up after she sets up the charitable annuity, she will still have made a good investment.

Canada Pension Plan provides a death benefit. Ask contributors to include a provision in their will directing their executor to apply for the benefit and donate it to your fund.

Permission to use the following chart has been provided with the courtesy of Royal Bank of Canada[11]:

Personal and Estate Planning Considerations in Charitable Giving

Donation Option	Minimum Amount Required?	Can You Revoke The Gift?	Do You Get Income Or Use During Lifetime?	Subject To Probate?	Charitable Tax Credit Usable?	When Can Charity Use The Gift?
Outright gift now	None	No	No	No	Now	Immediately
Bequest under will	None	Yes, by changing your will prior to your death.	Yes	Yes	After death in your final tax return	After death
Insurance Policy: *Charity is owner & beneficiary of policy	Check with charity	No. If you don't pay premiums, charity can pay them, reduce death benefits, or cash in policy	No.	No	Now and as you pay future premiums	After death. Can borrow on policy now.
*Charity is beneficiary of policy only	Check with charity	Yes, as owner of policy you can change beneficiary of policy.	Yes, if you can cash in the policy, but then there's nothing left for the charity.	No	No amount qualifies for a charitable tax credit	After death

---

[11] Royal Bank of Canada. (1994). *Planned Giving.* Toronto: Royal Bank of Canada.

Charitable gift annuity	Depends on issuer	No	Periodic payout is virtually tax-free if you're 70+	No	Now but granted only if you take reduced annuity payments	After death
Charitable remainder trust (inter vivos trust)	$100,000 – enough to justify required legal/trust fees	No	You can use property and receive all income generated	No	Now based on gift value adjusted for your life expectancy	After death of life tenant (income beneficiary)
Endowment fund	Depends on Purpose	No	No	Only if gift made under your will	Now, or on death for gift under will	Immediately
Private charitable foundation	Several hundred thousand dollars. Creation & operation requires professional services.	You can fund it with a loan to be repaid if needed. Loan can be forgiven at death or if no money needed.	No, although you can control the investments & disbursements	Only if gift made under your will	For year of donation to foundation. No credit for a loan.	You control the grants subject to minimum yearly quotas set by tax rules

Various Types of Gifts	Lifetime Income to You	Tax Benefit
Bequest in your Will	No	Tax credit for estate to be passed on to heirs
Gift Annuity	Yes	Possible immediate tax credit and a portion of the income may be tax free
Remainder Trust	Yes	Large one-time tax credit
Stripped Bond	No	Large one-time tax credit
Life Insurance (new policy)	No	Tax credit on premiums
Life Insurance (existing policy)	No	Tax credit on cash value
Appreciated Securities	No	Immediate tax credit and reduced capital gains

Note: Generally, only money earned in Canada by foreign residents can be tax deducted as a charitable donation by the resident. Therefore, a friend or relative in the USA cannot donate to a Canadian charity and use the income tax receipt on their American tax returns unless those funds were earned in Canada. The charity usually has to qualify in the resident's own country as a charity.

Special Donation Projects

Special donation projects are ways to help people give in relatively small, consistent ways to an organization or family trust. These types of donations are based upon working with donors who are family members, friends, neighbours, colleagues, acquaintances and people interested in your fund.

Named fund Sometimes you will find a donor who wants to make a substantial contribution to your fund if you will allow them to name the fund after them or in honour/memory of a loved one. (See the Chapter 1 on General Information for more details on how to do the math for this option so you can have several or many funds.)

Bricks and mortar People often find it easier to donate when they know their name will be attached to a building, book, or something equally 'permanent'. That is why capital campaigns (to raise capital to build something or buy equipment) are called 'bricks and mortar' campaigns.

Another version of this method is to commission an artist to paint a scene whereby donors contribute to the 'bricks' within the painting. The 'brick' could literally be bricks within a building or home; or it could be leaves on a tree, flowers in a garden or dots. Each 'brick' is worth 'x' dollars. Let us use the example of a fund that requires $1,000,000. You can easily multiply or divide this example to reflect your needs (i.e., if you need $5,000,000, multiply example by 5; if you need $250,000, divide by 4). The RCMP have recently used this process to raise funds for an endowment that will preserve their vessel that was the first to go through the Northwest Passage declaring Canadian sovereignty over the north. In their case, they were selling a portion of the large mural that will be painted behind the ship.

Assume each brick costs $1,000. You will need to 'sell' 1,000 bricks. Each contributor gets a print of the painting, signed by the artist. Those who buy more than one brick can receive more prints, if they wish, or keep just the one.

A thousand dollars sounds like a lot but it is really only $40 per month for 2 years, or the price of a monthly movie for two with a few snacks. If they are contributing to a registered charity, they will, of course, receive a rebate of part of their contribution through a charitable receipt so your request is for even less money.

By encouraging the sale of 'bricks' you allow people the opportunity to contribute for only a two-year period with funds that will last forever in an endowment or trust fund. Some people can contribute the full amount at once while others will use the monthly deduction from their VISA or MASTERCARD or through pre-authorized withdrawals from their chequing account so the giving becomes 'painless'. Local business and larger corporations can be asked for a one-time contribution to the fund with a promise that you will never return to them for funds again. You can ask them to purchase one, several, ten or more bricks based on their interest in your fund and their capability to donate. Of course, you will keep them informed regularly of how the fund is used so they might contribute again without being asked.

If you need 1,000 bricks and you have 10 people sitting around the table with their contact lists, then you can almost guarantee that each person can personally contribute and get contributions for a total of 10 bricks each. That is 10% of your fund within the first few years, if everyone contributes monthly. If you raise nothing else for 10 years you will have doubled your investment. If you have a longer period of time then that, $100,000 will become $1,000,000 within about 30-35 years. That sounds like a long time until you realize that if you are creating a trust for a dependent child who is now 5, then you will have your fund by the time they are 40. Not many people are millionaires by the time they are 40. If you also factor in a life insurance policy by grandparents or parents and other wise investments, you will have your target long before the person becomes 40.

Small not-for-profit organizations and charities which want an endowment fund to cover operational costs will want a larger fund more quickly, perhaps, than for an individual trust. The principles, however, are the same. You break down the total need into manageable units and 'sell' those units. You may already have a donor base from which to work. Your network may already be larger than a family establishing a trust. Your purpose and values may be easier to 'market' to this network while providing your donors with tax advantages. You will also help your donors understand that their contributions will lead to long-term stability and accountability for the organization. Every other fund raising method can be tied to this one as each bake sale, auction, campaign drive can be recalculated into 'bricks'.

Another method of selling 'bricks' is to involve one's own union or community group to ask for 'x' dollars (low figure) per member for a one-time donation in return for offering to help establish a similar process for other members' favourite trust or endowment funds so that the membership appreciates they are contributing to funds that have life-long (and beyond) positive benefits.

Borrowing money to create a fund You may have identified a person on your contact list who has an excellent, personal or corporate credit rating. You approach this person with the following plan.

Let us assume, again that you need a fund of $1,000,000. This person or company would borrow 'x' dollars to invest for a limited time, e.g., 10 years. Their credit rating must be below what is normally available. They give the funds to you, or they invest it themselves (they probably have more experience), with the following conditions:

1. The principle funds remain untouched for 10 years.

2. The interest on the loan comes out of the investment earnings.

3. The difference between interest earned and interest paid off to the loaner remains in the fund for 10 years.

4. If the interest on the loan at any period during the 10 years is larger than the interest earned, the difference comes out of the fund's accumulated interest or principle. Alternatively, the person or company may wish to guarantee losses themselves and declare the loss on their personal or corporate income tax return.

5. At the end of 10 years, the loan is paid off in full and the accumulated interest is contributed to your fund.

6. The person or company who borrowed on your behalf will not have to contribute any of their own money. The lender has received the same return on investment as they normally would lending money to this person or company. The fund receives sufficient dollars to secure some financial security. Everyone wins!

Let's put numbers to this example. The fixed interest rate on the loan is 4%. The conservative estimate of return on investing the funds is 7%. The difference is 3% minus any fees. At that interest rate, it would take about 25 years to double the fund. We have only 10 years on this arrangement.

Therefore we will need about $3,000.000 in the fund. At the end of 10 years, the net interest will be about $1 million. Remember, no one losses money or uses their own assets to secure this fund. You are using a bank or other lender's money. With this option, you can continue with your regular fund raising efforts for annual operating costs and, after 10 years, you will have sufficient funds to operate without further fund raising.

Note: The above example would work just as well for a person who wants to use their own assets rather than borrowing funds. The difference would be that they would only have to contribute $1,000,000 to the fund as all the interest would accumulate over the 10 years and the money would double. They would lose out only on the interest of their investment and get their principle back. Such a person might decide that this method was an excellent way to make a long-term difference to several of their favourite charities. They might decide to set aside $1 million dollars to help 3 charities over the next 30 years (they could include provisions in their will to that effect). After helping 3 separate charities over 30 years, the funds could be contributed to a 4th charity as part of their estate planning. Such a person need not be exceedingly wealthy. As David Chilton wrote in *The Wealthy Barber*, there are many people in modest homes who have accumulated a substantial amount of money through conservative, long-term financial planning. They probably have their name in your address book right now!

Product sales Aside from 'selling bricks and mortar' you may want to consider writing a book, creating or producing a CD with music or poems, helping the person who needs the trust to prepare their autobiography, etc. The types of items you produce are endless. If they are inspirational and a good gift for people to give to their loved ones at Christmas, for birthdays or anniversaries; all the better. You produce them (or have the production donated) and sell the product, with a charitable receipt for the difference between cost and sale, to raise part of the endowment costs.

For example, Frank has a health condition that means he will probably die in the next few years. He is a bachelor. He wants to create a trust for his sister's daughter who has Down Syndrome. He has led a life of adventure and spiritual searching and wants to record some of those stories on a videocassette including some music he has written. He has also been inspired by his niece's quest to live a full life in her community and with the gifts she has to offer. He also wants to record the stories of some of the people who have accepted her gifts and who have thrived on their mutual friendship.

Frank has a high school buddy who now owns a small recording studio. He gets his friend excited about this project. Together they produce a 25-minute videotape and call it *Frank's Inspiration.* Frank makes a determined effort to sell copies of his tape for $25 to all of his family, friends, work colleagues, as well as to local schools, churches, community groups, cable TV, etc. who might find the stories interesting and helpful in some way. Each tape costs $5 to copy and produce a nice cover. He sells 200 copies and earns $4,000. The tape also asks people to contribute to the trust fund. He receives another $1,000. A few people are inspired by Frank's story and his efforts to help his niece enjoy the full richness of her life. They ask if they can help sell tapes for him now. They also want his permission to add an epilogue after his death and continue to sell the tape for his niece. They sell a further 200 tapes. That collected donation is now $9,000 and is in the Trust Fund. She is 15 years old. By the time she is 45, the fund will likely be worth over $72,000. At that time, she could use the funds as a down payment on her own home.

To take the example further, if Frank wanted to help even more, he could have named his niece as his beneficiary of his term insurance policy. When he died, she could inherit, for example, $100,000. Leaving it in the fund until she was 45 would mean an accumulated wealth of about $800,000. Together with his product sales she could begin taking out the interest from the fund of about $59,500 per year or take out whatever principle she might need; e.g., to buy a home.

Another example comes from Carberry, Manitoba where volunteers planted, maintained and cultivated a 40-acre field of potatoes for two seasons netting more than $80,000 to create a community foundation endowment fund.

Several groups helping raise money for each other's funds In some cultures, children within a family help each other buy a home. The oldest child gets the pooled resources of all the children to buy the first home and so on. Often, the older children will have the younger children live in their homes rent free so they can help save up for the next house to be bought. In each case, the home is bought without a mortgage to the great savings of each child. For example, a home that costs $200,000 will end up costing closer to $500,000 after a 25-year mortgage is paid off.

Endowment and trust funds may require a minimum contribution (e.g., $10,000) to start a fund. Small not-for-profit and charitable organizations as well as families setting up trust funds can do something similar to the families described above. By pooling their resources, their network of interested family and friends, etc. they can pool sufficient principle to establish a fund for one of them first, then the next, etc. Pulling names out of a hat would be one way to choose the order in which funds are opened. The people's whose funds are opened first will be earning interest first and a portion of that can be contributed to the next fund to be set up. Through thoughtful planning and a contract between families or groups, everyone can begin a fund sooner than they thought possible.

The family cottage When parents die leaving the family cottage to the children to continue traditions that bind families together, they also leave behind a debt. Upon the death of the first or second parent, there is a capital gains tax payable as if the cottage was sold and paid out of the children's inheritance. Using good estate planning, these parents can give their children the cottage and give a large donation to their favourite charity.

An alternative is to buy an insurance policy on a joint last-to-die basis which will pay out at about the same time as the capital gains tax is payable. The beneficiary is the estate of the last-to-die parent and through that person's will, the proceeds of the insurance go to the charity of choice. The receipt will be for the amount of the gift.

Sherry Kushner and Ed Pearce give the following example from their article, *Planned Giving and the Family Cottage* (1997).

A couple, aged 65, owns a cottage worth about $120,000. Their adjusted cost base (ACB or what the cottage cost them originally in present dollars) is $50,000. They need to calculate what the cottage will be worth, allowing for inflation, to their best statistical mortality. Using 3% (low for vacation property) and 25 years, the fair market value (FMV) at the 'deemed disposition' when both parents are dead is estimated at $250,000.

Cottage FMV	$250,000	Insurance	$150,000
ACB	$50,000	Annual Premium	$3,666
Capital Gain	$200,000	Pay Period	10 years
Taxable Gain (75%)	$150,000	Total Cost	$36,660
Tax Payable (50%)	$75,000	Tax Savings*	$75,000

*The proceeds of the life insurance will produce a tax receipt for the estate of $150,000 (the gift to the charity). At a 50% fax rate, the receipt would save the estate approximately $75,000 in taxes which the estate then pays for capital gains tax on the cottage. The state gets its tax. The family get their cottage without decreasing the value of their inheritance. The charity gets a donation more than twice the size of the premium costs to the parents (therefore, a bigger donation than the family could otherwise make). The parents feel they have organized their estate so that everyone wins, including themselves.

Asking People to Give

Some tips on asking people to give large sums to your fund:

1. Know your stuff. Spend time within your group coming up with all the questions likely to be asked of you, and generate standard replies that you can modify as needed. Record the standard replies in typical day-to-day, conversational language. You will not read out your answers so they must feel natural to you.

2. Help people to share your enthusiasm and trust in the positive consequences of contributing to your fund. Understand the person's present connection, if any, to your family or organization. For example, you must know if they were active members 10 years ago or recently; regular contributors or one large donation 3 years ago.

3. When possible, the asker should have a similar background, age and experience of the person being asked. A doctor asking a doctor is more likely to succeed just as a senior talking with a senior. They will understand the person's questions more fully and give more appropriate answers.

4. Choose whether one or more of you should attend any face-to-face conversations depending on the person's level of comfort and trust. Rehearse your presentation, your asking and your answers to their questions to feel comfortable with what you are saying. Rehearsing is not about becoming a professional speaker or sale representative with a 'pat' sales pitch. Rehearsing is about becoming more comfortable in what you say and how you say it so that the person you are talking to is also more comfortable.

5. People only hear 20% of what you say and forget 80% of it within 24 hours. Have written or video material that details the specifics of what you are suggesting or asking for. Either bring it with you, or bring it by the next day to show you care that they are truly informed.

6. Schedule appointments by telephone rather than by mail. You might send a preliminary letter outlining your request for an appointment, but call to set the actual date and time. Do the calling yourself, rather than a secretary or other person. Build rapport as soon as you can.

7. Schedule appointments that fit the person's agenda, not yours. Meet them where they prefer, whether that be at home, office or elsewhere.

8. Ask for a specific amount of money or a specific method of donation. This requires some research as to what may be possible and requires some time with the person to see what might be realistic. Be patient. The longer rapport is built up the more committed the person may be to your fund.

9. Do not ask for a donation by telephone if you can avoid it. Meet the person personally and work out the details personally. You are building a long-term relationship, where possible, and personal contact will bring better mutual rewards.

10. Encourage a donor to use an independent lawyer with tax and estate planning expertise. Never let it be said that you coerced a person, without proper independent advice, to contribute to your fund. With large contributions, especially those given through wills, you want to minimize any legal problems with heirs or beneficiaries.

Appendices

Part 1: For Both Trust and Endowment Funds

Appendix A
Comparing Trust or Endowment Funds

(Copy out this form, one per organization you are checking out, to compare their services and fees.)

Institution Name and Contact Person

Telephone Number

Needs	Y	Advantages	Disadvantages	Fees
Assistance with creation of fund?				
Samples of forms and documents to evaluate?				
In-house trust or endowment managers?				
Staff willing to sit on advisory?				
List of satisfied customers?				

Needs	**Y**	**Advantages**	**Disadvantages**	**Fees**
Detailed accounting of fees and expenses?				
Other information?				

Appendix B
Specific Wording for Donations to Charities Through a Will

The following is specific wording your lawyer may suggest to include in your personal will or a donor's will. The sample clauses were prepared by Jim Hilbourne for the *Canadian Association on Charitable Gifts* in his November 4, 1998 article in *Canadian FundRaiser.* We are grateful for permission to reproduce it here.

1. Capital bequest with unrestricted use:

I direct my Estate Trustee to transfer as a gift to [Charity] the sum of ______ (or ______% of my estate or residue of my estate), to be used for such purposes in connection with the work of [Charity] as the Board of Directors may from time to time determine.

2. Capital bequest with restricted use:

I direct my Estate Trustee to transfer as a gift to [Charity] the sum of $______ (or _____% of my estate or residue of my estate), to be used for.

3. Endowment income with unrestricted use:

I direct my Estate Trustee to transfer as a gift to [Charity] the sum of ______ (or ______% of my estate or residue of my estate), to be held in trust for at least 10 years and kept invested and the income from which shall be used for such purposes in connection with the work of [Charity] as the Board of Directors may from time to time determine.

4. Endowment income with restricted use:

I direct my Estate Trustee to transfer as a gift to [Charity] the sum of $_____ (or _____% of my estate or residue of *my estate), to be held in trust for at least 10 years and kept invested and the income from which shall be used for__________.*

5. Reversionary bequest with unrestricted use:

I direct my Estate Trustee to transfer as a gift to [Charity] any bequest or residuary gift contained in this will to any charitable organization or institution or to any person or persons in trust for such organization or institution that cannot take effect in whole or in part because of any legal prohibition or because of the inability of any such organization or institution to take the gift for any reason whatsoever. Such gift is to be used for such purposes in connection with the work of [Charity] as the Board of Directors may from time to time determine.

6. Contingent bequest with unrestricted use:

If any of the beneficiaries names in this will should die before becoming entitled to receive their distributive share of my estate, I direct my Estate Trustee to transfer the share to which such beneficiary would otherwise have entitled to [Charity] to be used for such purposes in connection with the work of [Charity] as the Board of Directors may from time to time determine.

7. Specific property bequest:

I direct my Estate Trustee to transfer to [Charity] my [specific property].

8. Registered funds bequest with unrestricted use:

I direct my Estate Trustee to transfer to [Charity] the sum of $_____ (or _____% or all of any assets which I may own) which are registered either as a RRSP or RRIF, to be used for such purposes in connection *with the work of [Charity] as the Board of Directors may from time to time determine.*

9. Registered funds bequest with restrictions:

I direct my Estate Trustee to transfer to [Charity] the sum of $_____ (or_____% or all of any assets which I may own) which are registered either as a RRSP or RRIF, to be used for.

10. Power to vary purpose clause:

(This clause empowers a charity to vary the purposes for which a gift is used if circumstances make it impossible or impracticable to carry out the original wishes or purposes of the donor. It is recommended that this clause be used whenever a restricted or designated gift is made.)

If, in the opinion of [Charity's] Board of Directors, it should become impossible, inadvisable or impracticable to apply the said bequest's funds or income for the said purposes, the Board of Directors shall use the said bequest or such part thereof in such manner as in its discretion may seem to be to the best advantage of [Charity] for other purposes related as closely as possible to the spirit and intention of this gift. However, if in the opinion of the Board of Directors it is impossible, inadvisable or impracticable to utilize the said or such part thereof for such related purposes, then the Board of Directors shall use the said bequest or such part thereof for such other purposes of [Charity] as the Board of Directors may determine.

11. (Not in original by Canadian Association on Charitable Gifts) Named endowment: Modify clauses above to permit a Charity to open up a named endowment in the name of the donor or other person as directed by the will but include the following provision in case the minimum to open a named endowment has increased since the person prepared their will.

I direct my Estate Trustee to open a named endowment fund with the transfer of $_____. If such amount is not sufficient to open a named endowment at the time of my death then I direct my Estate Trustee either: (a) add to the transferred funds from the remainder of my estate the amount required to open such a fund; OR *(b) instruct the charity to use the funds for a smaller named endowment or, if that is not possible, then the Board of Directors shall use the said bequest or such part thereof for their general endowment fund for such other purposes of [Charity] as the Board of Directors may determine. The Trustee has complete discretion to choose between option (a) or (b).*

Appendix C
Last Will and Testament and Settling the Estate

Wills are required in Canada if you want control over how your assets will be distributed after your death. Without a will, provincial law determines who will get what and how much will go to governments. To adequately plan for your financially dependent loved one's future finances, you must have a will.

This book is not a summary of preparing wills but this appendix should help you with the basics. The resources listed at the end of the book may lead you to other useful resources beyond your own lawyer. Always have a lawyer prepare your will to ensure all of your wishes are properly included.

Wills should be revised or rewritten if any of the following occurs:

- Separation or divorce.

- Death of a spouse, child, grandchild or other significant beneficiary as well as death of an executor, trustee or guardian.

- New marriage (existing will is invalid upon a marriage).

- Move to a new province or country.

- Long-term illness or disability of a child or grandchild (you may consider a trust fund for them).

- Changes in probate, estate planning, tax laws or regulations that affect your situation.

- Changes in beneficiaries.
- Increases or decreases in bequests to beneficiaries.
- Changes in the terms of testamentary trusts.

Choosing an Executor

An executor is someone will have to handle all of the financial and legal affairs after the person(s) named in the will dies. Choose one, or several people to handle these affairs. Make sure they are willing to do this work as it can be time consuming and frustrating dealing with all the bureaucracies involved. You may choose a family member or friend to be the executor with, or without, the assistance of a lawyer to handle most of the paper work.

Executor's Responsibilities

The Executor will need a copy of the will and the ability to get at the original to settle your estate. They should meet with the deceased person's lawyer, if any, and with co-executors to divide the work. They should begin to record the costs of getting professional help that will be paid out of the estate.

The Executor must generally:

- Help with arranging the funeral, as required by the family, including notifying others of the death.

- Contact the deceased main bank, trust or credit union to provide money for the family's immediate living expenses. **Note**: Do not make any disbursements listed in the will until you know there will sufficient assets to settle all debts, including income taxes.

After the immediate needs are met, they should:

- Decide whether probate is necessary, i.e., in very modest estates a will may not have to be probated. However, if property or other larger assets are involved, the will must be probated.

Probating a will involves presenting formal proof before the proper officer or court that a person's will is their true last will and confirms the executor(s) named in the will. The executor receives a *Grant of Probate*, also called *Grant of Letters Probate* and *Letters Probate*, known in Ontario as *Certificate of Appointment of Estate Trustee with a Will.* In Quebec, probate is only applicable for a will not in notarial form.

Not all wills require probate. If you are the executor, check with your provincial regulations and/or an estate lawyer to help you through this process.

If probate is necessary: (a) make an application to the court to probate the will (or have a lawyer do this for you) and (b) upon receiving 'Letters Probate' from the court stating that the last will and testament is approved by the court and you are the executor, you may begin to deal with the assets and liabilities as required by the will and by law. For example, you will need notarized copies of the probate papers to access assets in banks and trusts.

- Locate and record vital information including the original will; names, addresses, birth dates, contact numbers and e-mails for the deceased, immediate family, deceased person's parents and siblings; beneficiaries in the will, on RRSPs, and on insurance policies.

- Identify, record and protect all assets and liabilities of the estate including all cash, jewellery, collectibles, deeds, securities, stock certificates, mortgages, insurance policies, business interests, debts owed to the deceased, debts of the deceased, other liabilities and to secure, protect, insure and/or store assets as required. Write out the appropriate information for each to identify them completely. Notify the property insurance company of your efforts to ensure proper coverage. **Note**: Jointly held property or bank accounts, some insurance policies and trusts are usually outside the estate process and should not be identified as part of a person's estate for probate purposes. However, they should be identified and located for record keeping purposes.

- Make a list of the assets and liabilities of any business (including farms, self-employed businesses and partnerships) using the business's accountant to help you. Either help keep the business going (as per the will) or shut it down using the help of professionals and/or business partners as necessary.

- Contact all banks, trust and credit unions regarding the deceased (including joint account holders) and close all solely owned accounts. You will probably also need to open a separate account in the name of the estate to cash cheques and make payments including income taxes, credit card balances, outstanding bills, and to pay for expenses such as the funeral, legal fees, accountant's fees, etc.

- Locate all safety deposit boxes, itemize the contents of and disperse contents according to the will, and then close the boxes.

- Claim benefits from life insurance policies, veteran's affairs, Canada Pension, company and/or pension benefits and outstanding salaries.

- Advertise, if necessary, in appropriate newspapers to try and locate people or organizations owed money from the estate. Pay these debts out of the estate once all claims are in and you have verified the accuracy of the claims.

- Notify the post office to re-address the mail as well as notify all organizations and individuals who send correspondence or bills to the deceased (utilities, telephone, cable, credit card companies, driver's license, provincial government offices including health, driver's license, insurance companies, charities, associations and professional affiliations the deceased had, unions, catalogue companies, Internet providers, newspaper and magazine subscriptions, etc.)

- Cancel all credit cards after paying off the balance and destroy the cards.

- Sell off undistributed assets as per instructions in the will or based on your authorized judgment and distribute profits accordingly.

- Verify ownership of any homes, cottages, mortgages, cars, etc. Pay off outstanding debts including taxes and utility costs. Make sure properties remain insured until they are either transferred to heirs or sold.

- Have the person's accountant prepare their last income tax return or do it yourself if the estate is small.

- Disburse the estate's assets keeping detailed and accurate records. You may need to:

    a) Notify beneficiaries of what they will receive.

    b) Distribute bequests after all debts and other charges accounted for, and obtain releases from further liability from named beneficiaries.

    c) Make interim distribution to residual beneficiaries such as charities.

    d) Convey, sell or hold assets not specifically bequeathed such as real estate, automobiles, furniture, and securities until final distribution.

    e) Set up trust funds as directed in the will.

    f) Have a final sale of unbequeathed assets.

    g) Have a final clearance from Canada Customs and Revenue Agency that all income taxes have been paid.

    h) Have a final distribution of the estate.

    i) Notify family members and professional advisors once estate is distributed.

- Have a complete accounting of your administration of the estate and all fees incurred including your own fee and/or expense as Executor (perhaps described within the will).

If there is no will or an invalid will then:

1. Provincial laws will determine who are the heirs and what portion of the estate they will get through their *intestate succession* laws. The division differs between provinces but is divided, according to formulae, between spouse and children. If there are no spouse and children it usually goes, in order, to: parents; if neither parents survives, to brothers/sisters; if none survive to nephews/ nieces; if none survive to other next of kin; if none traceable**, it all goes to the government**.

2. The Court in your province will appoint an administrator (often a spouse or adult child) to take care of the estate who may not be a person you would choose.

3. The distribution of the estate may be delayed while an administrator is appointed and familiarizes themself with the estate.

4. The provincial court will appoint a guardian for your minor children who may not be someone you would have chosen. The court will also decide the children's inheritance. If there are difficulties in your family, your children may be placed outside your family while a decision about guardianship is made.

5. Your estate may lose a significant portion of its assets through federal and provincial taxes.

So, once again, it is best to plan ahead by making a will to ensure your loved ones' financial future is secure.

Appendices

Part 2: Trusts

Appendix D
Sample Discretionary Trust Created by a Last Will and Testament

The following is the sample of the Last Will and Testament of Susan Vivas (described in Chapter 7). It is presented here as an example of what your lawyer may include in your will to create a discretionary trust.

(Do not copy this will for yourself. Get legal advice from an experienced lawyer in these matters to prepare or change your own will to meet your own needs.)

Last Will and Testament of Susan Vivas. [We have removed only the standard opening of name, place and revocation of previous wills to save space.]

TRUSTEES

2. I APPOINT my husband, Johan Vivas, to be the sole Executor and Trustee of this my Will, provided that if my husband should die either in my lifetime or after my death but before the trusts hereof shall have terminated, or should refuse or be unable to act or to continue to act or should by deed resign as my Executor and Trustee, then I APPOINT Thomas Freeman *[younger family friend]* and Julia St. Laurent *[neighbour]* and Wilma Homings *[niece]* to be the Executors and trustees of this my Will in the place and stead of my husband and I declare that the expression "my Trustees" used throughout this my Will shall include, where the context permits, the Trustee or Trustees for the time being of this my Will, whether singular or plural.

DISPOSITION OF ASSETS CONTROLLED BY THE TRUSTEES

3. I GIVE the whole of my property, both real and personal of whatever kind and wherever situate, including any property over which I may have a general power of appointment, to my Trustees upon the following trusts:

Expenses and Death Taxes

(a) I DIRECT my Trustees to pay out of and charge to the capital of my general estate, my just debts, funeral and testamentary expenses and all succession duties and estate, inheritance and death taxes, whether imposed by this or any other jurisdiction whatsoever that may be payable to connection with any property passing on my death, and I hereby authorize my Trustees in their uncontrolled discretion to elect to defer payment of any such taxes or duties or to commute or prepay any such taxes or duties. Any duties or taxes so paid shall be treated as an ordinary debt of my estate.

Residue

(b) To pay or transfer the residue of my estate to my husband, Johan Vivas, if he survives me for a period of thirty (30) days. Notwithstanding the foregoing condition of survivorship, during the said period, my husband shall have the use of all articles of personal, domestic, household and garden use or ornament belonging to me at my death, including consumable stores and including all automobiles, snowmobiles, boats, motors, other vehicles and accessories thereto, and my Trustees may pay to or for my husband such amount or amounts out of the capital of my estate as they in their absolute discretion consider advisable without him being bound to the repayment thereof under any circumstances.

(c) If my husband should not survive me for a period of thirty (30) days, to dispose of the residue of my estate as follows:

Household Goods and Personal Effects

(i) To give to such of my children, Jessie Vivas and Mark Vivas who survive me such articles of personal, domestic, household and garden use or ornament belonging to me at my death, including consumable stores, which they wish to have or, if they cannot agree, as my Trustees in their absolute discretion determine, knowing that my children or my Trustees as the case may be will give effect to any wishes I may have expressed verbally or in writing with respect to the disposition of the said articles or any of them. Any of the said articles which shall be undisposed of in accordance with the foregoing provisions shall be sold by my Trustees upon such terms and conditions as they in their absolute discretion determine and the proceeds of any such sale shall fall into and form part of the residue of my estate, or such articles shall be given to such one or more charitable organizations as my Trustees in their absolute discretion determine.

Legacies

(ii) To pay to my daughter, Jessie Vivas, and my son, Mark Vivas, if they survive me the following legacies as soon as conveniently possible after my death, the sum of Five Thousand Dollars ($5,000.00) each.

Residue

(iii) If my children, Jessie Vivas and Mark Vivas or either of them survive me, I DIRECT my Trustees to set aside and keep invested the residue of my estate for my said children and during the lifetime of my said children my Trustees shall keep such residue invested and pay any amount or amounts or the whole of the annual net income therefrom together with any amount or amounts or the whole of the capital thereof to or for the benefit of either or both of my said children as my Trustees shall, in the exercise of an absolute and unfettered discretion, consider advisable from time to time. Any income not so paid in any year in accordance with the foregoing provisions shall be accumulated by my Trustees and added to the capital of such residue, provided, however, that after the expiration of a period of twenty-one (21) years after the date of my death, the whole of the said income each year shall be paid to or for the benefit of any one or more of my issue who shall be alive at the end of each such year in such proportions and in such manner as my Trustees in their absolute discretion determine, and in default of such determination in any year, or to the extent such determination does not extend or take effect, to those of my issue alive at the end of each year in equal shares per stirpes. I declare that the capital of such share and the income therefrom shall not vest in my said children and the only interest my said children shall have therein shall be the payments actually made to or for the benefit of each such child therefrom. Without in any way binding the discretion of my Trustees I further declare that it is my wish that in exercising their discretion in accordance with the provisions of this paragraph, my Trustees shall take account of and, insofar as they consider it advisable, take such steps as will maximize the benefits my said children would receive from other sources including governmental sources if payments from the income and capital of my estate were not paid to or for the benefit of my said children, or if such payments were limited as to amount or time. In order to maximize such benefits, I specifically authorize my Trustees to make payments varying in amount and at such time or times as my Trustees in the exercise of an absolute discretion consider advisable. I expressly declare that my Trustees shall not be required to maintain an even hand between the income beneficiaries and the capital beneficiaries when investing and administering such residue, but may in their absolute discretion favour one class of beneficiary over another.

Without in any way restricting the exercise by my Trustees of the discretion herein given to them, and without imposing a legal obligation upon them, I declare it is my wish that in making decisions concerning payments to or expenditures on behalf of my children, Jessie Vivas and Mark Vivas that my Trustees consult with and be guided by the recommendations of an Advisory Board. The Advisory Board shall consist of my Trustees and the following persons who shall be living from time to time:

Rosalie Vacance, Tamara Christians, Albertus Trentiem, Jacqueline Sante and James Sydney and any other person or persons appointed to the Advisory Board by the Advisory Board.

I further declare that it is my wish that my Trustees consult with the said Advisory Board as often as may reasonably be required but at least four times a year with respect to the arrangements to be made for the care of daughter, Jessie Vivas, from time to time and before encroaching on the capital of such residue for the benefit of either of my children and before making any payments of capital or income directly to my children and either of them for their own use. It is my wish that one of my Trustees act as the Chairperson of the Advisory Board and that my Trustees be receptive to all constructive suggestions and advice which the Advisory Board may provide to them from time to time with respect to any matter concerning the welfare and well-being of my children.

I AUTHORIZE and DIRECT my Trustees to pay an honorarium of $250.00 to each member of the Advisory Board (including themselves) each year who attend a majority of the meetings held by the Advisory Board in such year. I further AUTHORIZE and DIRECT that, if it is determined that my daughter, Jessie Vivas, could benefit from having the assistance of a companion to live with, my Trustees may make such payments towards the salary and expenses of such companion as they consider advisable.

Upon the death of each of my said children, my Trustees shall pay out of the capital of such residue, such part or the whole of the expenses of such child's last illness and the burial expenses of my said child as my Trustees in their discretion consider advisable. Upon the death of the survivor of my said children, my Trustees shall divide such residue then remaining among my issue then alive in equal shares per stirpes.

<u>Share for Grandchildren</u>

(iv) If in accordance with the provisions of this my Will any grandchild of mine should be entitled to any part or parts of my estate, such part or parts (hereinafter referred to collectively as the 'share' of such grandchild) shall be held by my Trustees upon the following trusts:

My trustees shall keep such share invested and, until such grandchild shall attain the age of eighteen (18) years, shall accumulate and add to the capital of such share the annual net income derived therefrom, provided that notwithstanding anything to the contrary hereinbefore contained. I authorize my Trustees to pay to or from the benefit of such grandchild the whole or any part of the said annual net income in any year that they in their absolute discretion consider advisable until such grandchild attains the age of eighteen (18) years; and thereafter the annual net income from such share shall be paid to such grandchild until he or she attains the age of twenty-five (25) years, when such share then remaining shall be paid or transferred to such grandchild. Provided that my Trustees may at any time or times pay to or for the benefit of such grandchild any amount or amounts or the whole of the capital of such share as my Trustees in their absolute discretion consider advisable, provided further that if at the expiration of a period of twenty-one (21) years from the death of the last survivor of my issue born in my lifetime such grandchild should be under the age of twenty-five (25) years then, notwithstanding the foregoing provisions, the share held in trust for such grandchild or the amount thereof then remaining shall forthwith be paid or transferred to such grandchild for his or her own use absolutely. If such grandchild should die before becoming entitled to receive his or her share in my estate, such share or the amount thereof remaining shall be held by my Trustees in trust for the issue of such grandchild who survive him or her in equal shares per stirpes. If such grandchild should leave no issue him or her surviving, such share or the amount thereof remaining shall be divided among my issue who are the issue of the parent of such deceased grandchild who is a child of mine alive at the death of such grandchild in equal shares per stirpes or, if no such issue should then be living, among my issue alive at the death of such grandchild in equal shares per stirpes and held upon the same trusts as are herein provided for such issue.

Gift Over

(d) If at the death of the last to die of my husband, my issue and me the residue of my estate or any portion thereof should be undisposed of in accordance with the foregoing provisions, I DIRECT my Trustees to divide such residue of my estate or portion thereof to such one or more charitable organizations as my Trustees in their absolute discretion determine.

POWERS TO TRUSTEES

4. IN ADDITION TO ALL OTHER POWERS conferred on my Trustees by this my Will or by any statute or law, my Trustees shall have the following powers:

(a) IF ANY PERSON should become entitled indefeasibly to any share in my estate before attaining the age of majority, the share of such person and any income derived therefrom shall be held and kept invested by my Trustees, and the income and capital, or so much thereof as my Trustees in their absolute discretion consider necessary or advisable, shall be used for the benefit of such person until he or she attains the age of majority.

(b) I AUTHORIZE my Trustees to make any payments or transfers for any person under the age of majority or otherwise under a disability to a parent or guardian or person acting as such of such person, whose receipt shall be a sufficient discharge of my Trustees in respect of such payments. I expressly authorize the parent or guardian or person acting as such of any person under the age of majority or otherwise under a disability to make any election or elections on behalf of such person for the purposes of the Income Tax Act (Canada) or any similar legislation of any province or other jurisdiction in force from time to time.

(c) MY TRUSTEES SHALL USE their discretion in the realization of my estate, with power to my Trustees to sell, call in and convert into money any part of my estate not consisting of money at such time or times, in such manner and upon such terms, and either for cash or credit, or for part cash and part credit, as my Trustees in their uncontrolled discretion decide upon, or to postpone such conversation of my estate or any part or parts thereof for such length of time as my Trustees may thing best, and I hereby declare that my

Trustees may retain any portion of my estate in the form in which it may be at my death for such length of time as my Trustees in their discretion deem advisable (notwithstanding that it may not be in the form of an investment in which trustees are authorized to invest trust funds and whether or not there is a liability attached to any such portion of my estate) and my Trustees shall not be held responsible for any loss that may happen to my estate by reason of their so doing. No reversionary or future interest shall be sold prior to falling into possession unless my Trustees in their absolute discretion see special reasons for such sale and no property not in fact producing income shall be treated as producing income. Without restricting the general power and discretion herein given to my Trustees, I authorize and empower my Trustees to retain as an investment of my estate, for such length of time as in their absolution discretion they deem advisable, my interest in any business or businesses in which I may hold an interest at the time of my death and I give to my Trustees full power and authority to do all things which in their discretion they deem advisable in connection with any such business or businesses to the full extent that I could do if living.

(d) I DECLARE that my Trustees when making investments for my estate shall not be limited to investments authorized by law for trustees but may make any investments which in their uncontrolled discretion they consider to be to the advantage of my estate and my Trustees shall not be liable for any loss that may happen to my estate in connection with any such investments made by them in good faith.

(e) I AUTHORIZE AND EMPOWER my Trustees to deal with any securities, share or other interest of or in any syndicate, organization, company or corporation which shall be from time to time held by my Trustees, to the same extent and as fully as I could if I were alive and the sole owner of such interest, and in particular, without limiting the generality of the foregoing, to take up new or future shares, rights and interests, to join in plans for reconstruction or reorganization, to exchange shares, rights and interests and to give, receive accept and exercise options and to pay out of my estate any moneys which may be necessary for any of the purposes aforesaid. I also authorize my Trustees to retain as an investment of my estate for such length of time as in their discretion they deem advisable any assets or other interest whatsoever acquired by my Trustees through the exercise of the powers hereinbefore given to them.

(f) I GIVE TO MY TRUSTEES absolute discretion from time to time and at any time or times to make or not to make any election or elections, determinations, distributions and/or allocations for the purposes of the Income Tax Act (Canada) or any similar legislation of any province or other jurisdiction in force from time to time as my Trustees in their absolute discretion deem to be in the best interests of my estate and/or the beneficiaries, whether or not such election or elections, determinations, distributions and/or allocations may or would have the effect of conferring an advantage on any one or more of the beneficiaries or could otherwise be considered but for the foregoing as not being an impartial exercise by my Trustees of their duties hereunder or as not being the maintaining of an even hand among the beneficiaries. Where any specific funds, shares or residue are created under this my Will my Trustees shall form such fund, share or residue, as the case may be, unless otherwise expressly provided in my Will. I specifically exonerate my

Trustees from any responsibility with respect to any such elections, determination, distributions and/or allocations if they act bona fide in the exercise of such power.

(g) I AUTHORIZE my Trustees in their absolute discretion to sell, partition, exchange or otherwise dispose of the whole or any part of my real property in such manner at such time and upon such terms as to credit or otherwise as my Trustees in their discretion consider advisable, with power to accept purchase money mortgages for any part of the purchase or exchange price and to let or lease any real or leasehold property forming part of my estate, from month to month, or from year to year or for any term of years, subject to such covenants and conditions as they shall think fit, to accept surrenders of leases and tenancies, to expend money in repairs, improvements and, generally, to manage any such property. My Trustees shall also have the right to renew and keep renewed any mortgage or mortgages upon any real estate forming part of my estate, or any part thereof, to borrow money on such real estate upon the security of any mortgage or mortgages, and to pay off any mortgage or mortgages which may be in existence at any time forming part of my estate.

(h) MY TRUSTEES may make any partition or appropriation of any real or personal property forming part of my estate in its then actual condition or state of investment as they in their absolute and uncontrolled discretion consider advisable in or towards satisfaction or payment of any share or interest in my estate and may charge any share or interest therein with sums by way of equality of partition. For the above purposes, my Trustees shall have the power to determine the value of my estate and any part or parts thereof in any manner my Trustees shall see fit. Any such value shall become final and binding upon all the beneficiaries of my estate, notwithstanding that one or more of my Trustees may be beneficially interested in the property or any part thereof so valuated.

(i) I AUTHORIZE AND EMPOWER MY TRUSTEES to lend the whole or any part of my estate upon any security which they may deem sufficient or upon no security whatever; to enter into guarantees or indemnifications for the benefit of the beneficiaries of this Will and persons, firms or corporations other than the beneficiaries of this my Will and to give security thereof as my Trustees may in their discretion decide; and to renew and keep renewed such guarantees and indemnifications as my Trustees see fit; to borrow money from themselves individually or from any individual, firm or corporation, either without security or upon the security of any property, real or personal, entrusted to them or from time to time held by them under this my Will, for such purposes and upon such terms and conditions as my Trustees shall deem advisable, and without limiting the generality of the foregoing, for the payment of taxes, debts, duties, legacies or expenses and to mortgage, pledge, hypothecate or otherwise encumber, any or all of such property to secure the repayment of money borrowed; and to extend or modify any such encumbrance.

(j) NOTWITHSTANDING any direction to my Trustees to pay all of my just debts, I authorize and empower my Trustees to make arrangements for the gradual liquidation of any liabilities owing by me at my death, including, without limiting the generality thereof, claims against my estate arising before or after my death under the Family Law Act, R.S.O. 1990, c.F.3, as from time to time amended, or any successor statute, and to compromise, settle, waive or pay any claims at any time owing to my estate, or which my estate may have against others, for such consideration or no consideration, and upon such terms and conditions all such claims if my Trustees deem same advisable, and I hereby specifically exonerate my Trustees in connection with any such settlements if they act bona fide.

(k) Any benefit, whether as to income or capital or both, or income from capital to which any person shall become entitled in accordance with the provisions of this my Will or any Codicil thereto, shall not fall into any community of property which may exist between any such person and his or her spouse and shall not form part of his or her net family property for any purpose or purposes of the Family Law Act, R.S.O. 1990, c.F.3 in the Province of Ontario and any amendments thereto or any successor legislation thereto or any similar legislation in any other jurisdiction, but shall remain the separate property of such person, free from the control of his or her spouse. The separate receipt of such person shall be a discharge to my Trustees in respect of any such payment.

(l) I AUTHORIZE any one or more of the beneficiaries of this my Will, (notwithstanding that such beneficiary or beneficiaries may be a Trustee or Trustees of this my Will), to purchase any part or parts of my estate, real or personal, either at public auction or by private contract, provided in the latter case that the sale shall be conducted by my Trustees (or by the disinterested Trustee or Trustees of this my Will in the event that a beneficiary or beneficiaries so purchasing is also a Trustee or Trustees of this my Will), and shall be at such price or prices and subject to such terms and conditions and either for cash or credit or for part cash and part credit as the Trustee or Trustees of this my Will conducting the sale shall consider fair and reasonable.

(m) MY TRUSTEES ARE HEREBY AUTHORIZED, if they so desire, to appoint an agent or agents (which without limiting the generality of the foregoing shall include a trust company, investment counsellor or investment counsellors, or chartered accountant or chartered accountants) to act as their agent or agents in respect of the administration of my estate assets or to keep estate accounts and records. My Trustees may from time to time in their discretion terminate any such appointment and appoint another agent or agents to so act. My Trustees are further authorized to fix the amount of any remuneration that shall be a charge upon my general estate and payable out of the capital or income thereof in such proportions as my Trustees from time to time decide upon. I hereby declare that the amount of any such remuneration shall be deducted from any compensation to which my Trustees may from time to time be otherwise entitled. In making any such arrangements as aforesaid I authorize my Trustees to place the investments comprising my estate assets or any of them in the custody of such agent or agents, to transfer such investments or any of them into an agency account with such agent or agents or its or their nominee, and to delegate to such agent and agents any or all of the discretionary powers herein given my Trustees with respect to the investment and management of my assets.

(n) I HEREBY DECLARE that my Trustees shall not be liable for any loss that may happen to my estate or to any beneficiary hereunder resulting from the exercise by my Trustees in good faith of any discretion given them in this my Will.

CHILDREN BORN OUTSIDE MARRIAGE

5. Any reference in this my Will or in any Codicil hereto to a person in terms of a relationship to another person determined by blood or marriage shall not include a person

born outside marriage nor a person who comes within the description traced through another person who was born outside marriage, provided that any person who has been legally adopted shall be regarded as having been born in lawful wedlock to his or her adopting parent and any person who is born outside marriage and whose natural parents subsequently marry shall be regarded as having been born in lawful wedlock.

TRUSTEES' COMPENSATION

6. MY TRUSTEES SHALL BE ENTITLED to receive reasonable compensation for their care, pains, trouble and responsibilities in and about the affairs of my estate and to be reimbursed for all expenses incurred by them provided that any Trustee, who is also a beneficiary, shall only be entitled to be reimbursed for expenses and to receive a reasonable per diem payment for time spent on the affairs of my estate. If the amount of compensation for my Trustees is approved by the Trustees and a majority of the adult beneficiaries under this my Will as at the date of payment, and provided there shall be at least one adult beneficiary, then the settlement of such compensation shall be final and binding upon all persons concerned in the administration of my estate. In the absence of agreement, compensation shall be determined by a Judge of the Court in the jurisdiction where my estate is situate.

I AUTHORIZE my Trustees from time to time to pay to themselves from the capital and income of my estate such reasonable amount or amounts for compensation at such reasonable intervals during any account period in my estate, subject to subsequent approval of such amount of amounts so paid by a Judge or Authorized Officer of the Court on any passing of accounts or audit of assets of my estate.

IN TESTIMONY WHEREOF I have to this my Last Will and Testament, written upon this and [number] preceding pages of paper, subscribed my name this [day] of [month], [year].

SIGNED, PUBLISHED AND DECLARED

by the said Testatrix,

as and for her Last Will and)

Testament, in the presence of)

us, both present at the same)

time, who at her request, in)

her presence, and in the presence)

of each other have hereunto)

subscribed our names as witnesses.)

WITNESSES (2) Name, Address, Occupation, and signature.

Appendix E
Life Planning Guide

Chapter 6 includes a life planning method centred on a person's unique gifts, needs and hopes. The following is an example of a life plan that organizes a person's legal, financial and medical information. This one was prepared by Richard Fee and edited by *The* "Special Needs" Planning Group. It is reprinted with permission.

Life Plan Guide

Prepared by: ________________________Date:

Relationship to individual with "Special Needs":

To Whom It May Concern,

(Answer those sections relevant to your child.)

Information About (Your Child's Name)

General Information

Name List the full name of your child. Also the name he or she likes to be called.

Numbers List the Social Insurance Number, Complete Address Town, County, Telephone Number for home and work, height weight, shoe size and clothing size.

More Details List your child's gender, fluent language and religion. Indicate whether your child is a Canadian Citizen.

Birth List your child's date and time of birth, as well as any complications. List your child's birth weight and place of birth as well as the city/town/country where he or she was raised.

Siblings List the complete names, addresses and phone numbers of all brothers and sisters.

Marital Status List the marital status of your son or daughter with a disability. If married, list the spouse's name, his or her date of birth, the names of any children and their dates of birth. Also list any previous marriages, as well as the names, addresses and phone numbers of the spouses and children from each marriage.

Other Relationships List the special friends and relatives that your child knows and likes. Describe the relationship.

Guardians Indicate whether any guardians have been appointed. List the name, address and phone number of each guardian and indicate whether that person is a guardian of the person or the guardian of the estate. If alternate guardians have been chosen, list their full names, addresses and phone numbers.

Trustee Indicate whether you have set up a discretionary trust for your child and list the names, address and phone number of each trustee including alternates.

Power of Attorney If anyone has power of attorney for your son or daughter, list the person's full name, address and phone number. Indicate whether this is an enduring power of attorney.

Final Arrangements Describe any arrangements that have been made for your child's funeral and burial. List the full names of companies or individuals, their addresses and phone numbers. Also list all the payments made and specify what is covered. Indicate location of any contracts or agreements.

Otherwise, indicate your preferences (in consultation with your son or daughter if appropriate) for cremation or burial. Should there be a church service? If the preference is for burial, what is the best site? Should there be a monument? If cremation is the choice, what should be done with the remains?

Medical History and Care

Diagnoses List the main diagnoses for your child's condition, such as autism, cerebral palsy, Down Syndrome, epilepsy, impairment due to age, learning disorder, developmental delay, neurological disorder, physical disabilities, psychiatric disorder or an undetermined problem.

Seizures Indicate the seizure history of your son or daughter: no seizures; no seizures in the past two years; seizures under control; seizures in the past two years, but not in the past year; or seizures currently.

Functioning Indicate your child's intellectual functioning level (mild, moderate, severe, profound, undetermined, etc.)

Vision Indicate the status of your child's vision: normal, normal with glasses, impaired, legally blind, without functioning vision, etc. List the date of the last eye test and what was listed on any prescription for eyeglasses.

Hearing Indicate the status of your child's hearing: normal, normal with a hearing aid, impaired, deaf, etc.

Speech Indicate the status of your child's speech: normal; impaired, yet understandable; requires sign language; requires use of a communication device; non communicative, etc.

Mobility Indicate the level of your child's mobility: normal; impaired, yet self ambulatory; requires some use of a wheelchair or other assistance; dependent on wheelchair or other assistance; without mobility, etc.

Blood List your child's blood type and any special problems concerning blood.

Regular Physicians List your child's regular physicians, including specialists. Include their full names, types of practice, addresses, phone numbers and the frequency and time of visits.

Previous Physicians List their full names, types of practice, addresses, phone numbers and the most commons reasons for which they were consulted. Describe any important findings or treatments.

Dentist List the full name, addresses and phone number of your child's dentist, as well as the frequency of exams. Indicate what special treatments or recommendations the dentist has made. Also list the best alternatives for dental care in case the current dentist is no longer available.

Nursing Needs Indicate your child's need for nursing care. List the reasons, procedures, nursing skills required, etc. Is this care usually provided at home, at a clinic or in a doctor's office. If appropriate, include the full names, addresses, phone numbers of any nurses that provide care on a regular basis.

Mental Health If your child has visited a psychiatrist, psychologist or mental health counsellor, list the name of each professional, the address and phone number as well as the frequency of the visits and the goals of the sessions.

Therapy Does your child go to therapy (physical, speech or occupational)? List the purpose of each type of therapy as well as the name, address and phone number of each therapist.

Diagnostic Testing List information about all diagnostic testing of your child in the past; the name of the individual and/or organization administering the test address, phone number, testing dates and the summary of the findings. How often do you recommend that diagnostic testing be done? Where?

Genetic Testing List the findings of all genetic testing of your child and relatives. Also list the name of the individual and/or organization performing the tests, address, phone number and the testing dates.

Immunizations List the type and date of all immunizations.

Diseases List all the childhood diseases and the date of their occurrence. List any other infectious disease your child has had in the past. List any infectious disease your child currently has. Has your child been diagnosed as a carrier for any disease or condition.

Allergies List all allergies and current treatments. Describe past treatments and their effectiveness.

Other Concerns Describe any special concerns your child has, such as bad reactions to the sun or getting staph infections if he/she gets to hot.

Hygiene Describe any helpful hygiene procedures such as cleaning wax out of the ears every few months or trimming toenails. Are these procedures currently done at home or by a doctor or other professional? What do you recommend for the future?

Operations List all of the operations and the dates and places of their occurrence.

Hospitalization List any other periods of hospitalization your child has had. List the people you recommend to monitor your child's voluntary or involuntary hospitalizations and to act as liaison with doctors.

Birth Control If your child uses any kind of birth control pill or device, list the type, dates used and doctor prescribing it.

Adaptive Devices Does your child need any adaptive or prosthetic device, such as glasses braces, shoes, hearing aids or artificial limbs? List the manufacturing company(s) or supplier(s).

Medication List all prescription medication currently being taken plus the dosage and purpose of each one. Describe your feelings about the medications. List any particular medications that have proven effective for particular problems that have occurred frequently in the past, and the doctor prescribing the medicine. List medications that have not worked well in the past and the reasons. Include medications that have caused allergic reactions.

Over the Counter Medication (OTC) List any over-the-counter medications that have proved helpful, such as vitamins or cold remedies. Describe the conditions helped by these remedies and the frequency of use.

Medication Monitoring Indicate whether your child needs someone to monitor the taking of medications or to apply ointments, etc. If so, who currently does this? What special qualifications would this person need?

Medication Procurement Does your child need someone to procure medications for him or her? If so, who?

Diet If your child has a special diet of any kind, please describe it in detail and indicate the reasons for the diet. If there is no special diet, you might want to include tips about what works well for avoiding weight gain and for following the general guidelines of a balanced, healthy diet. You might also describe the foods your child likes best and tell where the recipes can be found for favourite dishes.

Information About Parents

General Information List each parent's full name, social insurance number (SIN), complete address, phone numbers for work and home, date of birth, place of birth, city/town/country where raised, fluent languages, religion, blood type and number of siblings. Indicate whether he and she are Canadian Citizens.

Marital Status Indicate each parent's current marital status. If they are currently married, list the date of that marriage, and the number of children from that marriage. Also list the dates of any previous marriages; names of previous spouses; and names and birth dates of children from each marriage.

Family List the complete names of each parent's siblings and parents. For all those still living, list their addresses and phone numbers, as well as something about them, especially about their relationship to your disabled son or daughter.

Housing

Present Describe your child's current living situation and indicate its advantages and disadvantages.

Past Describe past living situations. What worked? What didn't work?

Future Describe in detail any plans that have been made for your child's future living situation. Describe your idea of the best living arrangement for your child at various ages or stage. Which of the following living arrangements would you prefer?

- A relative's home (which relative?)
- Supported independent living in an apartment or house with_____hours of supervision.
- A group home with no more than_____residents.
- A private group home (which one?)
- Foster care for a child.
- Adult foster care.
- Parent-owned housing with_____hours of supervision.
- Housing owned by your child with_____hours of supervision, etc.

Size Indicate the minimum and maximum sizes of any residential option that you consider suitable.

Adaptation Does the residence need to be adapted with ramps, grab bars or other assistive devices?

Favourites List the favourite possessions that your child definitely would want to have in any living arrangement.

Community List the types of places that would need to be conveniently reached from your child's home. Include favourite restaurants, shopping areas, recreation areas, libraries, museums, banks, etc.

Daily Living Skills

Individual Program Plan (IPP) Describe your child's current Individual Program Plan or similar provincially mandated planning document (or attach a copy here).

Current Activities Describe an average daily schedule. Also describe activities usually done on 'days off'.

Monitoring or Assistance Discuss thoroughly whether your child needs someone to monitor or help with the following items.

- Self-care skills like personal hygiene or dressing.
- Domestic activities like housekeeping, cooking, doing laundry or shopping for groceries and cleaning supplies.
- Transportation for daily commuting, recreational activities and emergencies.

- Reinforcement of social and interpersonal activities with others to develop social skills.

- Other areas.

Caregiver's Attitudes Describe how you would like caregivers to treat matters like sanitation, social skills (including table manners, appearance and relationships with the opposite sex). What values do you want caregivers to demonstrate.

Self Esteem Describe how you would best reinforce your child's self esteem, discussing how you use praise and realistic goal setting.

Sleep Habits How much sleep does your child require? Does he/she have any special sleep habits or methods of waking up?

Personal Finances Indicate whether you child need assistance with personal banking, bill payments and budgeting. If so, how much help is needed?

Allowance Indicate whether you recommend a personal allowance for your child. If so, how much? Also, list your recommendations about supervision of how the allowance is spent.

Education

Schools List the schools your child has attended at various ages and the level of education completed in each program. Include early intervention, day care and transition programs.

Current Programs List the specific programs, schools and teachers your child has now. Include addresses and phone numbers.

Academics Estimate the grade level of your child's academic skills in reading, writing, math, etc. List any special abilities.

Emphasis Describe the type of educational emphasis (such as academic, vocational or community based) that your child currently concentrates on. What do you think would be the best for the future?

Integration Describe the extent that your child has been in regular classes or schools during his or her education. What are your desires for the future? What kinds of undesirable conditions would alter those desires?

Day Program or Work

Present Describe your child's current day program and/or job.

Past Describe past experiences. What worked? What didn't? Why?

Future Discuss future objectives.

Assistance Indicate to what extent, if any, your child needs assistance in searching for a job, in being trained, in becoming motivated, and in receiving support or supervision on the job.

Leisure and Recreation

Structured Recreation Describe your child's structured recreational activities. List favourite activities and favourite people involved in each activity.

Unstructured Activities What are your child's favourite means of self expression, interests and skills (going to movies, listening to music, dancing, collecting baseball cards, roller skating, etc.)? List the favourite people involved in each activity.

Vacations Describe your child's favourite vacations. Who organizes them? How often do they occur, and when are they usually scheduled?

Fitness If your child participates in a fitness program, please describe the type of program, as well as details about where and when it takes place and who oversees it.

Religion

Faith Indicate which religion your child belongs to, if any. Indicate any particular denomination or church of which your child is a member.

Clergy List any religious leaders, ministers, priests or rabbis familiar with your child. Include the names of the churches, synagogues or religious organizations involved. List their addresses and phone numbers. Also indicate how often your child might like to be visited by these people.

Participation Estimate how frequently your child would like to participate in services and other activities of the church, synagogue or religious organization. Indicate how this might change over time. Also describe any big events in the past.

Rights and Values

Please list the rights and values that should be accorded your child. Here are some examples of what you might list:

- To be free from harm, physical restraint, isolation, abuse and excessive medication.
- To refuse behaviour modification techniques that may cause pain.
- To have age appropriate clothing and appearance.
- To have staff, if any, demonstrate respect and caring and to refrain from using demeaning language.

Other

Give an overview of your child's life and your feeling and vision about the future.

Describe anything else future caregivers and friends should know about your child.

Finances, Benefits and Services

Assets List the total assets your child has as of this date. Indicate how those assets are likely to change, if at all, in the future.

Cash Income List the various sources of income your child had last year. Include wages, government benefits, pension funds, trust income and other income. This might include Canada Pension Plan, Disability Benefit.

Services and Benefits List any other services or benefits your child receives. These might be special services for children at home; home help; employment assistance; housing assistance; legal assistance; library services; child special education; transportation assistance; and vocational rehabilitation services.

Gaps Indicate whether any services or benefits are needed but not being received by your child. Indicate whether plans exist to improve the current delivery of services or to obtain needed benefits.

Expenses List all expenses paid directly by your child in various categories, such as: housing, education, health care, recreation, and vocational training.

List all expenses paid directly by parents, guardians or trustees in various categories.

List estimates of all expenses paid by third parties such as; insurance companies, pay direct Health Plan or paying for residential services.

Changes Indicate how your child's financial picture would change if one or both parents died. Be sure to list any additional cash benefits your child would be entitled to. Also list any cash benefits your child might be eligible for.

The Paper Trail

Will Describe the location of any will for your child and provide the names, addresses and phone numbers of the lawyers involved and of the executors.

Safe-Deposit Box List any safe- deposit boxes owned by your child, the addresses of the depository, the contents and the name of any person who has the power of attorney to enter the box.

Life Insurance Describe any relevant life insurance, group or individual, on your child. List the face amount, the insurance company, policy number, beneficiaries and where the policy is kept. Indicate how this might change at the death of either parent. Contingent owner, loss of group coverage.

Burial Papers List the location of the documents of burial for your child, (deed to plot, instructions for burial, organ donations), the cemetery's addresses and the preferred funeral home.

Health Insurance Describe any relevant health insurance for your child, including hospital, major medical and accident insurance. List the type of coverage, the limit of benefits the insurance company, the policy number and the location of the policy.

Employment Saving Plans Describe any relevant employee savings plans for your child, including the employer's name, type of plan, value and date of valuation.

RRSPs Describe any RRSPs owned by your child. Indicate account numbers and financial institutions where invested. List any RRSPs owned by parents that can be transferred to the child at death of parent.

Income Tax Describe the relevant income tax information about your child. Indicate locations of the following papers; the records for the current year, the latest income tax return and its supporting documents and any earlier returns and documents if available.

Real Estate Describe the location of real estate records if your child plans to live in your home. Include the location of purchase records, deed, receipts for capital improvements, inventory of contents and property tax receipts.

Trust Describe any trusts established for your child. Include the type of trust; the names, addresses and phone numbers of all trustee's including alternates, and the recent value of the trust(s).

Advisors Name all advisors, such as lawyers, tax preparers, insurance agents or financial planners. List their addresses and phone numbers.

Other Describe the location of your child's guardianship papers; school records; phone number of current case workers, if any; copies of birth certificate; Family Benefit Allowance forms; information about Family Benefit Allowance and other government benefits including most recent completed application forms.

Father's Signature Date

Mother's Signature Date

Appendix F
A Sample of a Trust Funded Through Insurance Benefits

The following material was written by Graeme Treeby and Rodney Dunn of *The* "Special Needs" Planning Group **for residents of Ontario**, ©1997. It is partially reprinted here with permission. The complete guide is available from the organization. This organization does not hold itself out as legal advisors and strongly encourages prospective clients to use lawyers in drawing up their plans.

This package outlines one possible way to arrange for the financial security of a financially dependent loved one. We do not specifically endorse this, or any other, plan but include it in the appendix for illustrative and information purposes only.

One of the founders of this *The* "Special Needs" Planning Group is a parent of child with a developmental disability. He, and his colleagues, use the term "Special Children" and "Special Needs" to reflect their own preferences. You may use different terms but the processes included in their materials are the same.

The "Special Needs" Plan Description

Introduction

Why Do I Need a "Special Needs" Plan?

Normally, when a disabled person inherits money, it will become part of their Liquid Assets for the purpose of determining eligibility for the Ontario Disability Support Program. For a single person currently receiving ODSP, the current Ontario threshold amount of liquid assets is $5,000. If the "Special Needs" person has assets in excess of that amount, then the ODSP benefits can be terminated until those assets are spent down to the $5,000 level. Once they are spent down, the individual must reapply for benefits. Unfortunately, the re-application process can sometimes take several months. During this time, both funding and other benefits like the Drug Card and Dental Card will not be available to the individual. In addition, when a person receiving ODSP funding receives income from other sources, then the ODSP cheque is reduced dollar for dollar for the income received.

The problem is further aggravated by the fact that the Succession Law Reform Act in Ontario requires that parents make provisions in their Will for their disabled child who may be financially dependent on them for support. The parents' dilemma is; how do we provide a 'Quality Lifestyle' for our "Special Needs" Child without affecting the ODSP entitlements while at the same time satisfying the Laws of the Province?

The basic premise of the "Special Needs" Plan is to provide our "Special Children with the 'Quality of Life' that they deserve and are currently enjoying while at the same time protecting their entitlement to the Ontario Disability Support Program and other Government programs. These programs are based on the assumption that our children have very limited assets or income. In order to protect these entitlements, we must be certain that any planning steps that we take give the appearance of not causing our children to be wealthy.

At the same time, it is imperative that our children cannot outlive the benefits that they derive from our planning and as parents, we want to have Guarantees in place that will ensure that our wishes are carried out after we are no longer here to guide the process.

Finally, we must be aware of the impact of the Succession Law Reform Act that requires that parents of financially dependent children provide for those children after they are gone. We can accomplish all of the above mentioned desires through the use of a variety of techniques and legal instruments such as the Absolute Discretionary Trust (also referred as the Henson Trust), our Will, Power of Attorney, the Insurance Act and others.

The Beginning of the Process

To accomplish the above mentioned objectives, The "Special Needs" Planning Group has developed an enhanced program that will make use of these planning techniques and legal instruments to create and maintain a 'Quality Lifestyle' for our children.

The first part of the planning process is to identify areas that could be problematic. For example, you must be certain that existing insurance policies on the lives of the parents don't have the "Special Child" as beneficiary. Your "Special Children" mustn't have excessive cash values in their own insurance policies. You must ensure that your existing Wills, Powers of Attorney, RRSP Beneficiaries, Bank Accounts, Savings Bonds, and other detailed financial issues are consistent with ensuring your child's income is kept with your financial goals for your child.

The "Special Needs" Insurance Contract

The "Special Needs" Planning Group has negotiated a very specialized insurance agreement with the Insurance Company. Unlike most insurance policies which make lump sum payments to beneficiaries at the death of the insured person, we have succeeded in having the proceeds held 'On Deposit' within the Insurance Company when the parent or the last parent in the case of a Joint Last-to-Die plan, dies. By holding these funds on deposit, they come under the jurisdiction of the Federal Insurance Act. Part of the protection that the Insurance Act provides is that these funds on deposit are fully creditor proof and as such, nobody, not even the Federal Government, can attach them in settlement of a debt of the parent, the child or the trustee.

In addition to holding the proceeds of the "Special Needs" Plan on deposit, the Insurance Company has agreed to pay out the interest earned by these funds based on the higher of either the minimum guaranteed rate in the Flex Account at the time of application or the 5-year compound Guaranteed Interest Rate or equivalent offered by the company at the time of the parent's death. This rate will be adjusted every 5 years using the same rate guarantee. The interest amount will be paid to the Trustees of the Absolute Discretionary Trust which you, the parents of the "Special Child" have created in your Wills, for the entire lifetime of the "Special Child". In turn, this interest amount is to be used to provide Lifestyle purchases for that "Special Child". This payment option is **Guaranteed, in writing,** to continue until the "Special Child" eventually dies and at that time, the original capital amount will be paid out to whomever the parents wish; tax free.

We have chosen the 5-year rate to be the basis of the payments since it is higher than many other interest bearing vehicles and yet, it is a Guaranteed type of investment. Our plan also offers a minimum interest rate guarantee based on the minimum rates offered when you acquired your insurance contract. We have not chosen Mutual Fund type investment vehicles since by nature, they can not guarantee a positive earning each and every month. Sometimes they incur losses in a given month and if this were to occur in your plan, then the "Special Needs" Child may not have the money required to provide adequately for the Lifestyle that is desired in that month.

It was also pointed out that this holding of the proceeds 'On Deposit' and paying the 5-year GIC rate is not something that most insurance companies will do. We approached many of the Canadian Insurance Companies and most indicated that they would not be willing to participate in this arrangement. Therefore, in order for the Plan to work, it is imperative that our "Special Needs" Insurance Contract be established and maintained.

In order to satisfy the requirements of the Succession Law Reform Act, it has been argued that a portion of the estate of the "Special Needs" Child's parents should also be directed to the Discretionary Trust. It is believed that by doing this, the

Public Guardian's attention will be brought to the "Special Needs" Plan. This will demonstrate to the Public Guardian that the parents have indeed provided for the "Special Child" with a lifetime flow of cash from the plan and an emergency fund within the Discretionary Trust.

The role of the Trustee that the parents have appointed to manage the Discretionary Trust is greatly simplified through the "Special Needs" Plan. Instead of having a long list of duties relating to the investing and care giving to the Trust Fund, the Trustee's role is that of a 'spender'. It is their responsibility to ensure that the "Special Child" has the 'Quality of Life Things' that are required by the "Special Child". They don't have to spend their valuable time on managing and investing the Capital of the Trust Account. Further details regarding the duties of the Trustee are located in Section 2 of the "Special Needs" Plan.

As previously mentioned, the original capital amount of the "Special Needs" Insurance Contract is held 'On Deposit' within the Insurance Company. Once the "Special Child" has died, this original capital amount is available to be transferred to whomever the parents wish, on a Tax Free basis. Often this money is given to the Trustee, other siblings of the "Special Child", or a Charity, perhaps as a reward for years of service to the well being of the "Special Child".

The Will and the Absolute Discretionary Trust

The Absolute Discretionary Trust (often referred to as a Henson Trust or Discretionary Trust) is a specific type of trust agreement that parents normally set up in their Wills. It is a very carefully worded trust agreement based on the precedent setting 'Henson Decision' which had the final appeal dismissed in September of 1989. That court decision has provided parents and relatives of "Special Needs" people in Ontario with a vehicle by which they can provide inheritances to their children without having the ODSP (Ontario Disability Support Program) benefits terminated. This trust also allows you to describe how you will use the insurance benefits of our plan for the long-term financial assistance to your child.

Appendices

Part 3: Endowments

Appendix G
Plan for Establishing An Endowment Fund

The following checklist summarizes the steps necessary to open, maintain, manage and eventually close an endowment fund based on information presented in Chapter 11.

Steps	Specific Activity	Potential Ideas	Person Responsible and by what Date
1. Discuss endowment idea with Board			
2. Assign staff/volunteer time to research			
3. Board makes firm commitment to fund			
4. Create action plan			

Steps	Specific Activity	Potential Ideas	Person Responsible and by what Date
5. Recruit Board/ Advisory Members with special expertise and interest			
6. Determine if other sources of funding at risk if endowment created			
7. Policy statements for the fund	(a) Overall and specific purpose of the fund		
	(b) Name of the fund		
	(c) Type of fund (i.e., mixed portfolio or fixed income)		

Steps	Specific Activity	Potential Ideas	Person Responsible and by what Date
	(d) Financial objectives (e.g., Consumer Price Index)		
	(e) Spending rules incl. 10-year rule, 4.5% disbursement rule and other disbursement rules		
	(f) Structure of fund including named funds, value per unit, when donations accepted		
	(g) Decision-making structure & responsibilities		
	(h) How donations can be made & sample agreement		
	(i) Closing fund procedures		

Steps	Specific Activity	Potential Ideas	Person Responsible and by what Date
8. Policy statement that unexpected gifts go to endowment fund for minimum 10 years			
9. Create a separate foundation			
10. Research and choose advisors (e.g., financial planner, lawyer, accountant)			
11. Research and choose institution to house fund			

Steps	Specific Activity	Potential Ideas	Person Responsible and by what Date
12. Open fund if financially possible			
13. Prepare marketing material, pledge cards, etc.			
14. Identify prospective donor list	(a) Prepare list of people who have already put family/organization in their will		
	(b) Follow-up with past donors		
	(c) Identify potential new donors		
	(d) Become known to the estate and financial planners in your community		

Steps	Specific Activity	Potential Ideas	Person Responsible and by what Date
	(e) Provide 'Wills Clinic' as a community service		
	(f) Prepare script for approaching potential donors		
	(g) Review long-term donor relationship methods annually		
15. Regular evaluation of process, assets and future planning cycle			
Others:			

Appendix H
Sample Endowment Fund Policies

(Lorna Somers, co-author of *Planned Giving for Canadians* (1997) with Frank Minton, has given us permission to reprint the following sample. She can be reached at Somersmith Publishing (905) 689-2538).

ABC CHARITY

ENDOWMENT POLICIES

The investment objective of the ABC Charity is to enhance the value of the endowment portfolio and at the same time provide a dependable, increasing source of income, which will be used to support the operating budget of the Charity. The portfolio shall include both equities and fixed-income investments. The equities are designed to provide current income, growth of income, and appreciation of principal. The fixed-income investments are intended to provide a predictable and reliable source of interest income while reducing the volatility of the portfolio. Investments will be diversified in order to enhance return and reduce risk.

ESTABLISHMENT AND NAME OF THE FUND

That the ____________________ (name of bank, trust company, credit union, investment firm or other financial institution) be instructed to set up an account or term deposits under the name ________________ (name can either be simply the organization's name or another one chosen by the board).

FINANCIAL OBJECTIVE

Total return shall be the method of measuring the performance of the endowment. This refers to the combination of income (interest and dividends) and appreciation/depreciation of the fund's value for a certain period of time. The specific financial objective is for total return less expenses and distribution of income to equal or exceed the Consumer Price Index (CPI) for that period. Real growth is a measure of the extent to which total return, less expenses and distributions, exceeds the CPI. It is recognized that this objective will not be attained every year because of market fluctuations, but it is expected to be attained over a period of time.

SPENDING POLICY

Income (interest, dividends and net rents) from the endowment shall be distributed to the Charity not less often than annually, and such income shall be used for the charitable purposes designated by the donors or, if undesignated, at the discretion of the Charity.

All capital gains, realized and unrealized, shall be allocated to the principal of the endowment, and there shall be no encroachment on this principal except as may be necessary to satisfy the disbursement quota from a capital account.

NOTE: *The Charity may prefer to invest some of its funds in a quasi-endowment where it may expend capital as needed. It can do this with any funds not subject to the ten-year rule under Section 149.1(1)(e)(i) of the Income Tax Act, or even with those funds after the expiration of the ten-year period. The policies here presented presuppose that the Charity is establishing a pure endowment with the intention of spending income only.*

ASSET STRUCTURE

To facilitate investment and accounting the endowment shall function as a mutual fund. Each individually-named endowed fund shall hold units as part of the investment pool. The initial value of a unit shall be $10.00 and thereafter it will fluctuate with the changing market value of the investments held in the pool. The number of units assigned each fund shall change only when additions are made, usually by gifts. On the last day of each quarter, the unit value will be determined by dividing the total market value of the endowment pool by the number of units in the pool. On occasion, income may be capitalized and transferred to the principal of a fund.

When contributions for the endowment are received they shall be temporarily retained by the Charity in a holding account and added to the endowment on the first day of the following quarter. The number of units assigned shall be determined by dividing the amount of the addition by the unit value as of the end of the immediately preceding quarter.

The funds within the endowment shall consist of all individually-named funds and the general endowment.

INVESTMENT MANAGEMENT

The endowment shall be managed by the finance and investment committee of the board (or other committee to which this responsibility is delegated), whose responsibilities in the area of investment administration are as follows:

- To recommend to the board policies for the management of the endowment.
- To make recommendations to the board on the selection of portfolio managers.

- To determine how assets are to be allocated.
- To monitor the management of the endowment portfolio in order to enhance return and control risk, and to keep the board fully informed.

ASSET ALLOCATION

The monitoring and adjustment of the mix of assets among the investment classes is a major factor in achieving investment return. The finance and investment committee shall carefully review the mix of assets in the endowment and periodically make, or instruct the portfolio managers to make, transfers within the prescribed asset class limitations. Ordinarily 40-60 percent of the portfolio shall be invested in equities and the balance in fixed-income investments and cash equivalents.

PORTFOLIO MANAGERS

The board, upon the recommendation of the finance and investment committee, may appoint one or more portfolio managers and may allocate endowment assets among them in whatever proportion it deems appropriate. One or more managers shall be given responsibility for equity investments, and one or more for fixed-income investments, or any manager may be given responsibility for both.

MINIMUMS FOR DESIGNATED ENDOWMENTS

Any amount may be contributed for the general endowment or for any previously-established named endowment.

The minimum required to establish a named endowment, the income from which can be used at the discretion of the Charity, is currently $10,000.

Permissible named endowments for specific purposes and the current minimum contributions to establish them are listed on attached Schedule A. (*The Charity should attach its own menu of named funds to this document, e.g., the minimum required to establish a fund to support a specific program, specific job or activity.)*

A named endowment for a non-listed purpose may be established subject to the consent of the board. The amount required for such an endowment will depend on the objectives to be accomplished, and will be negotiated between the donor and appropriate representatives of the Charity.

EXECUTION OF ENDOWMENT AGREEMENTS

A named endowment can be established either by a lifetime gift or by bequest. When it is created by a lifetime gift the donor and officers of the Charity will sign an endowment agreement that sets forth the terms of the endowment. When the donor executes a will containing language directing that a named endowment be established, no other documentation is required.

Contributions for existing endowments or for the general endowment require only a transmittal letter or the correct bequest language stating the donor's intention.

Appendix I
Sample Endowment Fund Agreement

(Lorna Somers, co-author of *Planned Giving for Canadians* (1997) with Frank Minton, has given us permission to reprint the following sample).

1. Establishment

[Charity] (hereinafter 'the Charity') hereby agrees to establish the (name of fund as chosen by donor) ENDOWED FUND ('the Fund') per the terms of this agreement, to become effective when contributions for this Fund total at least $_____ *(insert the required minimum for the particular endowment being established).*

2. Purpose

The purpose of this Fund shall be:

(possible options)

"To support the general purposes and programs of the charity"

"To support_________________ program or, if program ends, to support the general purposes and programs of the charity"

"To provide funds for improving the general quality of life standards for (*specific person or groups of persons*)"

"To..." (*describe particular purpose other than one of the above options.*)

3. Donor(s)

State the name(s) of the primary donor(s), his/her/their affiliation with the Charity, why the Fund is being established and some brief biographical information about the donor(s). This is the only record that will endure, and it should be sufficient to memorialize the donor(s) and provide information for any future publication about the Charity's endowments.

4. Funding

This Endowment shall be funded with the following (*include all applicable items with as much detail as possible*):

1. A cash gift of $__________.
2. A gift of securities (or real property) valued at $__________. (If the value is unknown, the property may be described.)
3. A gift of the remainder interest in a charitable remainder trust executed on__________(*date*).
4. A gift of the residual interest in (*description of property*) executed on __________ (*date*).
5. The gift portion of a charitable gift annuity executed on_________ (*date*).
6. A life insurance policy assigned to the Charity__________ (*date*).
7. Any other gift or bequests that (*name*) or other person may designate for this purpose.
8. Additional gifts that the donors intend to complete by__________ (*date*) which, when added o the initial gift, total at least $__________.

5. Investment

The donor(s) intend(s) that the property contributed to this Fund, or other property substitute for it, shall be held and invested by the Charity as a permanent endowment unless the purpose is amended in accordance with Article 7, but in no case shall the contributed property, or property substituted for it, be held for a period of less than ten years, in accordance with Section 149.1(1)(e)(i) of the Income Tax Act.

The income earned on the endowment shall be used for the purposes authorized by this agreement. The investment, management and expenditure of all funds shall be in accordance with the Charity's policies and procedures.

6. Administration

The principal of this endowment shall be retained, administered and managed by the Charity. The distributed income shall be used for the purposes described in Article 2.

7. Amendment

This agreement may be amended by the mutual consent of the Charity and___________during (his/her/their) lifetime(s).

If changed circumstances should at some future time make it impractical to continue using the income from this endowment for the designated purpose, and the donor(s) either is (are) not living or not able to consent to an amendment, then the Charity may predesignate the purpose of the endowment income, providing that the Fund shall continue to bear the name(s) of________________ and the amended terms shall adhere as closely as possible to the donor(s)' original intent for this Fund.

Donor(s):

____

(Date)

For the Charity:

(Name and title of person empowered to sign for the Charity)

____

(Date)

Appendix J
Specific Sample Agreement Between ACT and The Toronto Community Foundation

The AIDS Committee of Toronto has generously given us permission to reprint their agreement with the Toronto Community Foundation that created their endowment fund.

August 26, 1997

The Board of Directors of the **AIDS Committee of Toronto**, having the power and authority has resolved to establish an endowment fund with the Community Foundation for Greater Toronto ('the Foundation') and encloses a cheque in the amount of $131,526.33, being the initial capital.

The terms of the fund shall be as follows:

1. The fund shall be known as the AIDS Committee of Toronto Endowment Fund.
2. The purposes of the Fund are to carry out our charitable purposes as more specifically set forth in our articles of incorporation.
3.

    a) The initial capital of the Fund and the initial value of any additions thereto shall be held by the Community Foundation for Greater Toronto for a minimum of 10 years and invested in accordance with the Foundation's Investment Policy, in effect from time to time. Investments may include investments in mutual funds or other forms of pooled investment funds.

b) At such time as the Foundation has established a segregated fund for purposes of making investments based on certain ethical criteria, the Board of Directors of the **AIDS Committee of Toronto** would have the option of requesting that the balance of the Fund be transferred to such segregated investment fund.

4. The Foundation will ensure that any additions to the Fund by anyone other than the **AIDS Committee of Toronto** will be subject to a direction that the initial value of such additions will be held for a minimum of 10 years.

5. For purposes of this agreement, the following terms shall have the following meanings:

   a) 'Administrative Fee' means the annual charge for administrative services of the Foundation, including the investment manager's fee, calculated in accordance with paragraph 8.

   b) 'Annual Distributable Earnings' means that portion of the Earnings determined by the Foundation to be available for distribution in each year.

   c) 'Capital' means the Initial Capital of the Fund plus the initial value of any additions plus all Earnings retained by the Foundation in accordance with paragraph 6.

d) 'Earnings' means all income, dividends and realized and unrealized capital gains net of capital losses of the Fund less the Administrative Fee.

6.

a) In each year the Foundation will determine the Annual Distributable Earnings, and shall advise the **AIDS Committee of Toronto** as soon as such determination has been made. The determination of Annual Distributable will be based on the Foundation's capital preservation policy in effect from time to time. The balance of the Earnings will be added to the Capital.

b) Distributions from Distributable Earnings shall be made, at least annually in accordance with the Foundation's disbursement policy in effect from time to time, to the **AIDS Committee of Toronto**, a registered charitable organization.

c) All distributions from the Annual Distributable Earnings will be identified as coming from the Fund.

7. In the event that the **AIDS Committee of Toronto** ceases to exist or ceases to be a registered charity under the provisions of the Income Tax Act, the Board of Directors of the Foundation shall apply the portion of the distribution of the Fund which would have been entitled to receive such analogous charitable purposes involving similar institutions or organizations as the Board of Directors of the Foundation may determine.

8. Or (Please see attachment #1 -- Dissolution Clause.

9. In any year, the Administrative Fee will not exceed 1.5% of the market value of the Fund and shall be determined in accordance with the administrative policy of the Foundation in effect from time to time.

10. Confirmation of the terms of the Fund by resolution of the Board of Directors of the Foundation shall constitute establishment of the Fund.

11. The Foundation will issue receipts in respect of all charitable donations received to the **AIDS Committee of Toronto Endowment Fund**, unless the donor does not require a receipt for income tax purposes.

We trust that the above will meet with your approval and with that of the Foundation's Board of Directors.

Yours sincerely,

AIDS Committee of Toronto

Signed by Executive Director and the Chair, Board of Directors

Dated this 04 day of September, 1997.

Accepted as of the date set forth above:

Community Foundation for Greater Toronto

Signed by President and Chief Executive Officer and the Chair, Board of Directors

Attachment #1

Article Eleven

Dissolution

11.01

In the event that the Corporation [ACT] dissolves, after payment of liabilities, all assets or the proceeds from the sale thereof shall be distributed to Ontario registered charities devoted to lesbian/gay health interests that serve the community in the Toronto area. The Board* will be responsible for ensuring the appropriate distribution of assets.

Note: *'The Board' refers to the Board of Directors of the AIDS Committee of Toronto.

Appendix K
Sample Donor Agreement to Contribute to an Endowment Fund

When a donor makes a large contribution to your endowment fund through an outright gift or irrevocable deferred gift (e.g., such as a life insurance policy), the donor and organization should have a signed agreement that will:

1. Identify and gratefully acknowledge the contribution and wishes of the donor (including, perhaps, a bit of biographical information about the donor for future members of the organization to better understand the donor, the heirs and the circumstances of the gift).

2. Clearly state the purpose and administration of the endowment fund.

3. Contain legal language that satisfied Canada Customs and Revenue Agency's 10-year distribution quota rule.

4. Allow donors to pledge future or ongoing gifts (e.g., monthly) for a determined or undetermined period.

5. Provide clauses that permit the organization to change restrictions if the original intent of the donor can no longer be met or if the organization's mission changes to meet current needs unforeseen at the time of the donation.

6. Provide an opportunity to amend the agreement at any time with the signed consent of both the donor and group.

7. Explanation of what will happen with the donation should the fund be closed.

If an agreement cannot be mutually signed, a letter or a person's will signed by the donor and containing the necessary instructions can be enough.

For example,

Our charity gratefully acknowledges the one-time, $10,000.00 contribution of Ms. Jane Smith. Ms. Smith has worked throughout her life to help people facing similar challenges as those people we serve. Ms. Smith has specifically instructed that her gift, or any property substituted thereof, be held by us for a period of 10 years or more within our general endowment fund with interest used to help us in our general work.

Our endowment fund is used to provide long-term operational costs in four key areas as outlined in our mission statement (attached). We are committed to staying small (i.e., operational budget less than $100,000, in 2001 dollars). The fund is administered through our Board of Directors and held within our Community Foundation fund.

Ms. Smith has agreed to allow the Board of Directors to direct her principle and interest to other future projects not covered within our present mission statement should the need be greater in one of those new areas.

Should either Ms. Smith or our organization like to change any part of this agreement, an amendment can be made with the signed consent of both parties.

Should our charity close its operations, its endowment fund, all the proceeds (principle and interest) will be donated to other small, not-for-profit and/or charitable organizations committed to staying small and working in similar areas of interest.

(Signed and dated by both parties.)

Appendix L
Draft Agreement among Deohaeko Families for the Creation, Maintenance and Dissolution of an Endowment Fund

<u>**Definitions**</u>

Deohaeko Deohaeko Support Network (Durham Region), Inc.

Board The Board of Deohaeko Support Network

Individuals People receiving financial, natural and support assistance from Deohaeko up to a maximum of 10 individuals

Families Families of individuals receiving direct support through Deohaeko; with a member/representative on the Board

Fund Deohaeko's endowment fund belongs to the organization and not the families while the actual assets in the fund are owned by the Durham Community Foundation

Named fund Within the Deohaeko fund, donors may build a 'named fund' after themselves or someone else to honour them. The named fund is a part of the Deohaeko fund which, in turn, is part of the Community Foundation of Durham Region fund.

CFDR Community Foundation of Durham Region

Overall and specific purposes of the fund

To provide a measure of financial independence for the support of individuals within Deohaeko Support Network through building a fund whose revenues will one day provide sufficient operational and support dollars to meet ongoing needs.

The endowment fund has been established to the benefit of up to 10 individuals including the 7 individuals receiving support at present. The other 3 are as yet unidentified but may include sons and daughters of past founding board members in good standing and may be added in the future upon the consensus of the Board.

Name of the fund

Deohaeko Support Network Endowment Fund

Location and type of fund (mixed portfolio)

The Board will place its fund with the Community Foundation of Durham Region (CFDR), which has a portfolio that includes both equities and fixed-income investments. The investments will be diversified to enhance return and reduce risk. Changing the location and type of fund will require an 80% majority vote of family representatives on the Board (one vote per family). Non-family Board representatives will advise but not vote on fund matters.

Financial objectives

The combination of income (interest and dividends) and appreciation/depreciation of the fund's value over time less expenses and distribution of income should equal or exceed the Consumer Price Index (CPI). Real growth is a measure of the extent to which total returns, less expenses and distributions, exceeds the CPI. We recognize that this objective will not be attained every year because of market fluctuations, but it is expected to be attained over a period of time.

Spending rules including 10-year rule, 4.5% disbursement rule

The fund will follow disbursement regulations and will adapt to legal changes set out by relevant legislation and regulations as required including:

All assets donated to the fund must be kept for a minimum of 10 years.

The fund will disperse 4.5% of its assets annually as required and may choose to contribute part or all of that disbursement back into the fund.

Disbursements received by Deohaeko from the fund will be divided by the same methods used to disburse all operating funds through Board allocations.

All capital gains shall be allocated to the principal of the fund until the family Board members decide otherwise by at least 80% vote and there shall be no encroachment on this principal except as required to satisfy the disbursement quota from a capital account.

Structure of fund including use of named funds, value per unit, when donations accepted/rejected

The fund shall function as a mutual fund consistent with Community Foundation investing.

Deohaeko will permit 'named funds' with a minimum contribution of $5,000 within 2 years to establish such a named fund. Revenues from named funds will be allocated in the same way as other revenues (i.e., at the discretion of the Board). A named fund can be established by a lifetime gift (both donor and Deohaeko sign an agreement) or by bequest (the Last Will and Testament is only documentation needed.)

The unit value of the fund will be determined by the CFDR.

Donations will be accepted any time and held until CFDR accepts them or contributions can be made directly to CFDR into Deohaeko's fund.

Deohaeko reserves the right to reject any donations from sources inconsistent with Deohaeko's mission and values and any tied donations that are inconsistent with its mission and values.

Decision-making structure and responsibilities

Decisions about the creation, maintenance and dissolution of the fund will remain with the Board requiring an 80% majority of families represented on the Board (i.e., not 80% of the quorum at a meeting but a full 80% of the family representatives on the Board). Non-family representatives on the Board will be involved in all discussions and provide their advice but will not vote on fund matters. **Changes to this agreement** would also require an 80% majority of family members on the Board. At all times, the Board will strive to reach consensus before proceeding to the 80% rule.

At present, **allocations** of operating dollars are agreed by unanimous consent of the Board based on individual support-dollar needs relative to the other individuals; on individual wishes and to help keep the Deohaeko vision alive. Allocations from the fund will be limited to Schedule A. Donors will not be able to make specific disbursements requests as part of their donation.

When consensus is not possible, major changes, allocations or decisions will require at least 80% majority of voting family members. If an 80% majority is not possible the decision will have to be postponed until such consensus is possible. An outside facilitator may be brought in to provide support to the Board in building such a consensus.

If 80% of the Board families cannot agree on minor administrative or allocation decisions, then a 2/3 majority of quorum at a meeting will be sufficient.

a) The Board will have an **advisory standing committee** of three Board members (not necessarily all family Board members) to deal with the day-to-day administration of the fund. This committee will include the Board's treasurer and will recommend the use of any external advisors including financial planners, lawyers and accountants and will advise on where the fund should be located. The Board will make all final decisions by passing appropriate motions. The Board's president and/or treasurer and/or designate will be the main liaison with the Community Foundation of Durham Region and other external institutions, organizations, and professionals.

b) The Board's **fundraising** efforts will include the Fund as a key funding tool for the long-term financial security of Deohaeko.

c) **Families** are expected to contribute to the development of the fund through whatever means possible in their circumstances including own contributions, requesting contributions from others, fundraising efforts of the Board, etc.

Family contributions to the fund do not affect decisions on how revenues from the funds will be allocated.

How donations can be made including sample agreement

When a donor makes a large contribution to our endowment fund through an outright gift or irrevocable deferred gift (e.g., such as a life insurance policy), the donor and organization will have a signed agreement. No donations can be tied to a specific allocation. See Attachment B for sample agreement.

Protocol for when a new family joins Deohaeko and its fund

Once a family has been approved by a consensus of the Board to join Deohaeko, they can benefit from the revenues generated by the fund. They will not be required to contribute a certain amount to the fund when joining Deohaeko but will be expected to help the fund grow through similar methods of other Deohaeko families to the best of their financial abilities.

Protocol for when an individual and/or family leaves Deohaeko

a) When an individual receiving support from Deohaeko leaves the Rougemount Co-Op **but remains** within the network, the individual is entitled to ongoing financial benefit from the fund as determined by the Board. If their representative on the Board is geographically unable to represent them, a substitute must be appointed which will be either a sitting or new Board member.

b) When an individual receiving support from Deohaeko continues in the network but **their family withdraws** from the network, the individual is entitled to ongoing financial benefit from the fund as determined by the Board. Their family representative on the Board will be replaced by either a sitting or new Board member. If the individual's family refuses to allow an alternate representative on the Board, the individual will no longer be entitled to any financial benefits, however, he or she may still receive other supports through Deohaeko.

c) When an **individual receiving support leaves** the network (by choice or through death) and their **family remains**, the remaining family members, upon a decision of the Board, may continue to receive non-financial support within the Network. If an individual dies, their estate or family have no entitlement to any revenues from the fund.

d) When an **individual** receiving support from Deohaeko and **their family withdraw** from the network, no financial benefits from the Fund will be allocated including any assets donated to the fund by the individual and/or their family, friends or others in their name.

e) If a **Deohaeko family member on the Board** fails to follow the fundamental principles of Deohaeko, and the conflict is unresolvable within a reasonable amount of time, they may be **asked to leave** the board by a minimum of 80% of the remaining voting families. The individual they represent will continue to be entitled to ongoing financial benefit from Deohaeko and from the fund as determined by the Board. Their family representative on the Board will be replaced by either a sitting or new Board member. If the individual's family refuses to allow an alternate representative on the Board, the individual will no longer be entitled to any financial benefits, however, he or she may still receive other supports through Deohaeko.

Closing fund procedures

The fund will close on an 80% majority vote of the family Board members with all remaining assets being transferred either:

a) To Deohaeko if permissible by law and if funds have been held for at least 10 years.

b) To a similarly-minded charitable organization to be determined by the Deohaeko.

Policy statement that unexpected gifts to Deohaeko go to the endowment fund for a minimum of 10 years

Deohaeko passed a motion on ______________________________ to the effect that all unexpected or untied donations will go into their endowment fund. They further decided that untied donations of less than $10,000 would have at least 75% go into the fund and gifts over $10,000 would be decided by at least an 80% decision of voting Board members.

Dealing with conflicts

If a family requests more than their normal allotment from the fund for their loved one without the individual's needs having changed dramatically, the Board will use the previous year's allotment as a guidepost.

If a family has an unresolvable personal conflict with the Board [i.e., not related to 10.(e) of this agreement] but they are unwilling to leave Deohaeko for financial reasons, the Board (as a whole) may remove the family member from the Board by an 80% vote and appoint a new representative for the individual from a sitting or new Board member. The individual would continue to receive support (financial and other) at the Board's discretion (80% majority vote). If the individual's family refuses to allow an alternate representative on the Board, the individual will no longer be entitled to any financial benefits, however, he or she may still receive other supports through Deohaeko.

This agreement shall be construed in accordance with the laws of the Province of Ontario.

We, the parents of NAMES, agree to the terms set forth in this contract dated this__________ day of __________ 2002.

SIGNATURES OF PARENTS:

SIGNATURE OF WITNESSES:

Schedule A

Revenues generated by the Fund can be allocated for:

1. Contributing back to the Fund to help the Fund grow.
2. Direct support dollars (must be covered first before other requests/needs are considered).
3. Co-ordinator(s) salaries.
4. Things not covered by health plans.
5. Fixed assets for individuals and/or Deohaeko.
6. Retreats, learning events and the development and/or acquisition of learning resources (books, tapes, etc.).
7. Costs of 'keeping the vision alive' including presentations; explaining our model to supporters, circles, siblings; keeping our story and history updated, web page, and looking to the future for new directions.
8. Helping an individual retain their home.
9. Acquiring personal items to enhance their lives.
10. Things or services that the Board deems necessary for the individual.

Revenues generated by the Fund cannot be allocated for:

1. Fixed assets or direct support dollars that serve to segregate individuals supported by Deohaeko (e.g., a van for use only by Deohaeko and the individuals it supports).

2. Funding to family members except in cases where a family member is required to provide extra, direct care which results in financial hardship (e.g., similar to how families outside Deohaeko may use direct funding dollars to allow a parent to stay home and care for their child).

3. Parental needs.

4. Paying siblings.

5. Congregated programs.

6. Exploitation of our children through advertising.

7. Political contributions.

8. Vacations (except funds to cover direct support dollars to a supporter accompanying an individual).

A minimum of 80% family voting members on the Board will be final in resolving conflicts on fund allocations consistent with the Board's mission, values and legal requirements.

Appendices

Part 4: Resources

Organizations and Useful Resources/References

List of Important Contact People

Each of the following professionals should have a specific expertise in estate planning, long-term financial planning, trusts and endowment creation and maintenance. The expertise required in these fields of law and investments is not something a professional can acquire quickly. If your own lawyer, banker, financial planner, or accountant have limited, recent expertise in these areas, ask them for a referral but do not let them 'learn as they go' with your financial future.

Financial Planner (list qualifications)

Lawyer (list qualifications)

Accountant (list qualifications)

Investment Firm Representative (list qualifications)

Third Party (e.g., Association for Community Living, a fund-raising association, a family group with special interest in long-term care of dependent loved ones)

This group may have either professional staff with expertise in meeting your long-term financial needs and/or members and volunteers with a personal expertise gained through personal experience that may be helpful to you. This group may also be able to recommend specific professionals whom they have entrusted with their investments. Regardless of their recommendations, shop around and compare to choose the best professionals for your specific needs.

Organizations

Canadian Association on Charitable Gifts, c/o CIMC, Suite 201, 1155 Young Street, Toronto, ON M4T 1W2. (416) 934-3424. **Finance@missioncanada.ca**. A national organization to assist charities in preparing consistent, standard gift annuities.

Canadian Center for Philanthropy is Canada's national fundraising membership organizations with resources, online database and publications including the *Front and Centre* newspaper. Suite 700, 425 University Avenue, Toronto, ON M5G 1T6. (800) 263 1178 or **www.ccp.ca**

Canada Customs and Revenue Agency (formerly Revenue Canada) has legal and regulatory information on their site about tax implications for individual donors and for not-for-profit and charitable organizations. **www.ccra-adrc.gc.ca/taxcredit/menu-e.html**. Its web site also has information on trusts and income tax returns for trusts **www.ccra-adrc.gc.ca/tax/trusts/menu-e.html**. Check this site for up-to-date information on taxation concerns for trusts.

Canadian Government's general site with links in all areas of taxation for charities and not-for-profits as well as on health, housing, legislation, and reports. **www.gc.ca**

Charity Village is a Mississauga, Ontario based not-for-profit whose web site is packed with helpful information for both donors and charities/not-for-profits alike. It provides career information, donor information and articles from various fund-raising journals that keep you up-to-date on issues relevant to those in the field. They are at: **www.charityvillage.com**

PLAN is a British Columbian based charity that provides information and support to families with disabled children especially in the areas of long-term life planning including estate planning, financial investments such as trusts and helping develop and maintain support networks. Boundary Plaza, Suite 260 - 3665 K, BC V5G 1G4. (604) 439 9566. **www.PLAN.ca**

Provincial governments have specific legislation on trusts, trustees, etc. Do a search at the following sites to get relevant information.

Alberta	**www.gov.ab.ca**
BC	**www.gov.bc.ca**
Manitoba	**www.gov.mb.ca**
New Brunswick	**www.gov.nb.ca**
Newfoundland & Labrador	**gov.nf.ca**
Northwest Territories	**www.gov.nt.ca**
Nova Scotia	**www.gov.ns.ca**
Nunavut	**www.gov.nv.ca**
Ontario	**www.gov.on.ca**
PEI	**www.gov.pe.ca**
Quebec	**www.gouv.qc.ca**
Saskatchewan	**www.gov.sk.ca**
Yukon	**gov.yk.ca**

The "Special Needs" Planning Group, whose resources have been reprinted in this book, are located at 70 Ivy Crescent, Stouffville, ON L4A 5A9. (905) 640-8285. **www.specialneedsplan.org**

Revenue Canada (see Canada Customs and Revenue Agency)

Community Foundations in Canada by Province

Note: Community Foundations do not have consistent policies across Canada. Get specific information from your local foundation to find out how it opens, maintains/manages and closes endowment funds.

Province	Community Foundations
Yukon (1)	The Yellowknife Community Foundation
British Columbia (27)	Abbotsford Foundation The Alberni Valley Community Foundation Bulkey Valley Foundation Campbell River Community Foundation Central Okanagan Community Foundation Comox Valley Community Foundation Coquitlam Foundation Kamloops Foundation Kent Harrison Foundation The Maple Ridge Community Foundation Mission Foundation Nanaimo Community Foundation North Shore Charitable Foundation Community Foundation of the South Okanagan (formerly Penticton & District Foundation) Parksville Qualicum Community Foundation Phoenix Foundation of the Boundary

Province	Community Foundations
	Communities Prince George Community Foundation Revelstoke Community Foundation The Richmond Foundation Salt Spring Island Foundation Shuswap Community Foundation Surrey Foundation Vancouver Foundation Vernon & District Foundation The Victoria Foundation The West Vancouver Foundation Community Foundation of Whistler
Alberta (9)	The Calgary Foundation The Greater Camrose Community Foundation Drayton Valley Community Foundation Edmonton Community Foundation Community Foundation of Greater Grande Prairie The Lethbridge Community Foundation Mayerthorpe Area Community Foundation Medicine Hat Community Foundation Red Deer & District Community Foundation
Manitoba (28)	Altona Community Foundation Inc. Beautiful Plains Community Foundation The Boissenvain & Morton Foundation Inc. Brandon Area Foundation Brokenhead River Community Foundation Inc. Carberry and Area Community Foundation Inc. Carman Area Foundation Inc. The Cartwright and Area Foundation Inc. Dauphin & District Community Foundation Inc.

Province	Community Foundations
	The Glenboro Area Foundation Inc. The Interlake Community Foundation The Killarney Foundation Inc. Morden Area Foundation North Norfolk - MacGregor Foundation Inc. Northern Neighbours Foundation Inc. Pembina Manitou Area Foundation Inc. Pilot Mound & District Foundation Portage & District Foundation Inc. Selkirk & District Community Foundation Souris Glenwood Foundation Inc. The Southwest Manitoba Regional Foundation Steinbach Community Foundation Thompson Community Foundation Tiger Hills Community Foundation Virden Area Foundation Inc. Westshore Community Foundation Winkler Community Foundation The Winnipeg Foundation
Ontario (24)	Aylmer Area Community Foundation Brantford Sesquicentennial Community Foundation Burlington Community Foundation Cambridge & North Dumfries Community Foundation The Chatham Kent Community Foundation The Community Foundation of Durham Region Guelph Community Foundation Hamilton Community Foundation Horonia Communities/Fondation communautaire de l'Huronie The Community Foundation of Greater Kingston

Province	Community Foundations
	The Kitchener and Waterloo Community Foundation London Community Foundation The Napanee District Charitable Foundation Community Foundation of Oakville The Community Foundation of Orillia & Area Community Foundation of Ottawa Owen Sound & Area Community Foundation The Sarnia Community Foundation The Town of Simcoe Foundation Sudbury Community Foundation Thunder Bay Foundation Toronto Community Foundation Tri-Town Foundation The Greater Windsor Community Foundation
Québec (1)	Fondation Communautaire du Grand Québec
New Brunswick (4)	Fredericton Foundation Inc. Fundy Community Foundation Community Foundation of Greater Moncton Inc. The Saint John Foundation
Nova Scotia (1)	The Halifax Foundation
Prince Edward Island (1)	Community Foundation of Prince Edward Island
Newfoundland (1)	Bonne Bay Community Health Foundation

Written Resources

The following references are only a few of the many useful resources that you can find in your local libraries, within your own organization, and in your local bookstores. Look for further books but also journal articles, magazine reports, films, videos and audiocassettes. Also keep in mind how much you can learn from experts in the field, including people within your own organization.

B.C. Civil Liberties Association. (1990). *Managing an endowment fund campaign: A handbook for non-profit organizations.* Vancouver: B.C. Civil Liberties Association.

Canadian Association on Charitable Gifts. (November 4, 1998). "Sample bequest wordings -- Let me count the ways..." in *Canadian FundRaiser* as reprinted by Charity Village, Mississauga, Ontario on their Web site: **www.charityvillage.com**

Canadian FundRaiser. (June 19, 1996). "Strip bonds: An attractive new vehicle for fundraisers" as reprinted by Charity Village, Mississauga, Ontario on their Web site: **www.charityvillage.com**

Chilton, David. (1989). *The wealthy barber: The common sense guide to successful financial planning.* Toronto: Stoddart.

Dickson, Mary Louise, Walsh, Rod, & Endicott, Orville. (1999). *The wills book: Benefits, wills, trusts and personal decisions involving people with disabilities in Ontario.* Toronto: Ontario Association for Community Living.

Foster, Sandra E. (1996). *You can't take it with you: The common-sense guide to estate planning for Canadians.* Toronto: John Wiley and Sons. She can be reached by fax at: (416) 642-3980 or at **web.idirect.com/~carat**

Gray, Douglas & Budd, John. (2000). *The Canadian guide to will and estate planning.* Toronto: McGraw-Hill Ryerson.

Klees, Janet. (1996). *We come bearing gifts.* Toronto: PSD Consultants. Klees presents the history of Deohaeko Support Network in Pickering, Ontario. This group of 10 families came together to secure the long-term social, housing and financial needs of their adult children with developmental disabilities. The book includes extensive discussions on the creation and maintenance of support circles.

Kushner, Sherry & Pearce, Ed. (July 2, 1997). "Planned giving and the family cottage" in *Canadian FundRaisers* reprinted by Charity Village, Mississauga, Ontario on their Web site: **www.charityvillage.com**

Minton, Frank & Somers, Lorna. (1997). *Planned giving for Canadians: A guide to institutions and managing a successful planed giving programme (2nd edition).* Waterdown, ON: Somersmith.

Morgan, Peter J. & Nemeth, Gerry. (1996). *Family trusts for tax and estate planning.* Vancouver, BC: Self-Counsel Press.

Nill, Stephen C. (April 13, 1996). "Planned giving aims to tap release of assets" in *Charity Village NewsWeek*, Mississauga, ON and available from their Web site at: **www.charityvillage.com**

Pearce, Dr. Edward. (September 5, 1994). "Let's take the mystery out of probate," in *Canadian FundRaiser* and reprinted with copyright protection by: Charity Village, Mississauga, ON from their Web site at **www.charityvillage.com**

Royal Trust. (1994). *Planned giving: Helping others while saving taxes.* Toronto: Royal Trust Corporation of Canada.

Stewart, Wayne. (May, 1994). "Endowment funds and the Community Foundation" in *Philanthropist,* Vol 12, No 1.

Vale, Norma. (March 1996). "More charities are considering setting up parallel foundations -- for a lot of good reasons" in *Front and Centre,* Vol. 3, No. 2.: p. 1, 16-17 by Canadian Centre for Philanthropy.

Glossary

The following list includes basic legal and financial definitions. For a complete definition use more extensive, standard legal and financial dictionaries.

adjusted cost base The cost of a capital property for tax purposes which may be above or below what one paid for it.

administrator The person appointed by the court to administer an estate when there is (a) no will, (b) no executor named in a will, or (c) named executor unwilling or unable to act.

affidavit A sworn statement in writing made before a lawyer or notary public.

alternative minimum tax A set of rules that limit the tax advantage that an individual can have in any given year from certain tax incentives such as RRSP contributions, capital gains and tax-shelter investments.

annuitant A person who receives a guaranteed income (e.g., from a charitable gift annuity, RIF).

annuity A sum of money is transferred to an annuity provider (e.g., bank, insurance company) and the provider makes periodic payments (e.g., monthly, quarterly, annually) to someone for a specified term.

assets Property and income owned by a person or corporation including real estate, other physical properties, cash, corporate shares, promissory note, trademark or copyright.

associate decision-maker A person who makes decisions on behalf of an adult with disabilities, with some input from the person. Person may also be called an *assistant decision-maker* or in Quebec, *adviser*.

beneficiary Person who receives a benefit from a will, insurance policy or trust fund. In the case of trusts, beneficiaries can benefit from the income of the trust (***income interest***), the capital (***capital interest***) or both.

bequest A gift made in a person's last will and testament. If making a charitable gift through a will, the person must write out the charity's full corporate name to prevent legal battles. For example, if making a gift to cancer, is the gift for the local, provincial or national cancer society in Canada or abroad; is the gift for the Cancer Society or for a research organization with cancer in its title or to a hospital specializing in cancer treatment?

capital The cash or property owned by a person or corporation including substituted property, realized capital gains and accumulated income. Usually distinct from interest earned on the capital that may be paid out to a beneficiary in a trust.

capital cost allowance The tax relief available on the depreciation or wear and tear over time on capital property such as manufacturing equipment, automobiles, and computers.

capital gain/loss The difference between a capital property's fair market value and its adjusted cost base -- essentially what you've made, or lost on an investment. For example, a share in a company cost you $10 three years ago and is now worth $15 when you sell it. The capital gain is $5.

capital interest Those capital assets that are contributed to a trust (e.g., cash, property) which is different than the income interest earned on those assets.

cash surrender value The amount paid by an insurance company if you cancel a life insurance policy. This is the money set aside within your policy to subsidize future premiums so that the policy's cost is level over the entire payment period. An over-simplified example is that your first few premiums might actually only be $200 for your age and health when you begin your policy. The actual cost of your last premiums should be $400 given that you are 20 years older and the cost of inflation on the value of your money. By averaging out at $300 per year, the insurance company invests the extra costs of the early premium to subsidize the greater costs at the end of the policy. When you cancel you policy, they give you a portion of that extra money back.

charitable gift annuity A life annuity issued by a charitable organization with funds donated by an individual (for tax as well as charitable purposes) which are expected to be greater than the annuity paid out regularly to the donor for life. Any capital in the account at death reverts to the charity for use in its charitable works.

charitable remainder trust A donor transfers ownership of property to a trust and names a charity as the capital beneficiary. While the donor is alive they, or another designated income beneficiary, can use the property and receive any income from it. After death, the charity is the sole beneficiary.

circle A group of people who are committed individuals who provide direction, encouragement, and support to an individual with disabilities or ongoing advocacy needs. Such circles may be relatively short term (e.g., a home care situation when someone is ill or recovering from debilitating treatments) to long term (e.g., around a person with an ongoing disability). See reference section for resources on creating, maintaining and encouraging such circles.

committee The legal term in BC, Manitoba, New Brunswick and PEI to describe the legal guardian of an adult with developmental or mental disabilities. *See also* ***guardian.***

creditor A person to whom money is due.

deemed disposition Canada Customs and Revenue Agency (formerly Revenue Canada) rules that deem you to have disposed of all of your assets on your death. Any capital gains are deemed to have occurred and taxed accordingly.

deferred gift A charitable donation arranged now for payment in the future, often after death.

dementia Deterioration of a person's mental capacity from changes in the brain.

discretionary trust fund (*See also* ***trust fund***) A trust that allows the trustee to be flexible in how, when and how much payments will be to, or for, the beneficiary, provided payments are made according to the terms of the trust.

disbursement quota A federal income tax rule requiring registered charities to spend in the present year 80% of the funds raised in the previous year, and for which income tax receipts were issued. This regulation is meant to ensure that most of a charity's funds are used for charitable purposes, that expenses are kept to a reasonable level and that excessive funds are not accumulated. Exceptions to the rule are made for bequests, gifts from a registered charity, and for donations made by donors who require the charity to hold the gift for at least 10 years (e.g., to be used in an endowment fund).

encroach (on capital) Paying out to a beneficiary portions of the money or other assets (capital) being held in trust. The trust agreement may allow the trustee to pay capital from the trust for general situations (e.g., 'for general benefit') or limited (e.g., 'for purchasing a home').

endowment fund A separate fund of money and assets that must be kept for at least 10 years. The interest from the money and assets may be dispersed (a minimum of 4.5% per year) but the principal cannot be touched. Endowment funds can hold money, stocks, mutual funds and bonds, property, and other physical assets. They are usually created to help fund a specific program or service or to donate to charitable organizations.

estate All the assets owned by a person at death which are governed by their will. Excluded from your estate are beneficiaries from insurance policies and trusts.

estate freeze A method of limiting the growth in value of a person's estate by diverting the growth, usually to the beneficiary. Therefore, parents may freeze their estate as of a certain date and any growth in its value will benefit their beneficiaries, usually their children.

even hand Trustees are to invest funds within a trust fairly and equitable so that all beneficiaries benefit equally from the decisions. For example, if a trust names one person the capital beneficiary and another person the income beneficiary, then the trustee cannot invest all assets in such a way that generates lots of income (benefits income beneficiary) but little appreciation to the assets themselves (hurts the capital beneficiary). Recurring and operating trust expenses are usually paid from trust income while major, permanent repairs or improvements to property are payable from capital. Depending on the ratio of these expenses, one beneficiary may benefit more than the other, which is considered inappropriate.

executor/executrix The man/woman or institution named in a will to administer an estate following the terms of the will and the legal requirements set out by provincial laws. In Ontario, the executor is known as the *estate trustee* and in Quebec the *liquidator.*

family trust Established for the sole benefit of family members including infant children and dependent elders.

fiduciary A relationship whereby one person holding legal title to assets through a trust acts in the best interest of the beneficiaries of that trust.

fair market value The price something would earn on the open market during a normal time period between a non-related buyer and seller.

gift in kind A gift of property other than money.

grant of probate *See also* ***probate.***

guardian The person(s) legally responsible for minor children or in Alberta, Saskatchewan, Ontario, Nova Scotia, PEI and Newfoundland, the person legally responsible for an adult with developmental or mental disabilities. In Quebec the term is *curator.*

hereditary Something inherited from parents.

incapable/incompetent Legal terms used to describe people deemed not able to understand the information that is relevant to making a decision and, therefore, not able to appreciate the "reasonable foreseeable consequences of the decision or lack of the decision". Each province has its own legal requirements for determining capability and competence.

indenture Also called ***trust deed.*** The terms and conditions of a trust either decided when opening a Living Trust or described in the Last Will and Testament of a settlor.

income The money (e.g., interest and dividends) generated on an ongoing basis through investments of capital.

income interest Income (e.g., cash, rent, dividends) earned from the capital within a trust or endowment.

instrument A written document such as a deed, will, trust, contract, lease or mortgage.

inter vivos trust *See also* ***life trust***

intestate A situation where a person dies without having a valid will. Partial intestacy occurs when a valid will does not deal with all of the estate's matters.

irrevocable gift or transfer A gift or transfer to a trust fund that cannot be taken back by the person making the gift or transfer.

issue All descendants from a common ancestor which includes children, grandchildren, great grandchildren, etc.

joint tenants A form of joint ownership where the death of one owner automatically transfers ownership to the other joint tenant(s) deemed to occur at the time of death.

Last Will and Testament *See also* ***will.***

life interest Also called ***life tenant*** receives the right to use a property for a specific period of time (often their lifetime) and upon their death the property title is given to another person. For example, a surviving spouse may have life interest in the family home until her death when it will be transferred to their child.

life tenant *See also* ***life interest.***

life trust Also called ***inter vivos trust*** is a trust created while the settlor is still alive.

mental incapacity *See also* ***incapable/incompetent.***

Non-discretionary trusts Established by settlors with clearly defined responsibilities outlined for the trustees including when and how beneficiaries can receive benefits, whether benefits include only income earned or also principle assets, and any specific limitations or requirements as defined by the settlor. For example, the parents may decide that only income earned in the trust can be given to the beneficiary except for the purchase of a home when principle may also be given out.

notarize A notary public authenticates or attests to the truth of a document (i.e., attests that a document was signed by a particular person).

notary public A public officer (can be a lawyer) who certifies documents, takes affidavits and administers oaths.

planned giving A charitable gift made in such a way that you maximize your tax and estate planning benefits. Once made, most of these donations cannot be taken back.

per stirpes The method of dividing assets of an estate if a beneficiary has died. For example, a grandparent may leave 10% of their estate to each child but one child has died, therefore, their children, if any, would divide that 10% equally among themselves.

personal property All property owned by a person except for real estate and buildings.

preferred beneficiary election Allows trust beneficiaries who receive tax credits for mental or physical disabilities to be taxed at their own income tax level (often little or no taxes due) and they can keep their trust income within the trust to accumulate up to their 21st birthday. Other people must have their trust income taxed at the tax bracket of the trust.

power of attorney A written document that allows a person to give someone they choose authority to act on their behalf in certain circumstances. Powers of attorney can be general or specific for such things as handling someone's financial matters (i.e., ***Power of Attorney for Finances***) or for health care decisions (i.e., ***Power of Attorney for Personal Care***). The person you designate can speak for you when you are unable due to illness or disability but you can revoke their power at any time verbally or in writing. The power of attorney stops immediately upon your death when your executor takes over decision making for your estate.

precatory trust Not a true trust but rather a settlor transferring ownership to a trustee who has absolute title to the property and free to dispose of it as they wish including for their own benefit. The settlor is relying on the trustworthiness of the recipient to carry out their wishes.

probate Formal proof before the proper officer or court that a person's will is their true last will and confirms the executor(s) named in the will. The executor receives a *Grant of Probate*, also called *Grant of Letters Probate* and *Letters Probate*, known in Ontario as *Certificate of Appointment of Estate Trustee with a Will*. In Quebec, probate is only applicable for a will not in notarial form.

proceeds of disposition The actual money earned from the sale of an asset (less expenses) or the deemed value when there is no actual sale.

property Tangible assets such as land, home, and collectibles (e.g., stamps, coins, antiques, art).

public trustee The provincial government official whose office supervises substitute decision-makers and guardians. In Quebec, the equivalent position is the *curator public* while guardianship appointments are known as *curatorships* or *tutorships*.

RRIF (Registered Retirement Income Fund) A formal plan, registered with Canada Customs and Revenue Agency, which is a tax shelter for funds transferred from an RRSP at maturity. The retired person draws regular income from the Fund and pays taxes only the amount withdrawn.

RRSP (Registered Retirement Savings Plan) A formal plan, registered with Canada Customs and Revenue Agency, which is a tax shelter for funds invested by the plan holder to accumulate savings and earnings for retirement, tax free. When the taxpayer reaches the age limit for RRSPs, the funds may be transferred into a RRIF or used to purchase a life or fixed term annuity to maintain the tax-sheltered status of the funds. If funds are removed for other purposes, they are taxed as income.

real property Land and buildings, also known as real estate or realty.

remainder interest That capital interest left over after the life interest beneficiary has died. This remainder interest is bequeathed in the trust to someone else. For example, a mother leaves the family home to her daughter (remainder man) in her will but the daughter can only claim the home after her father (life interest beneficiary or life tenant) dies. The father can live in the home for as long as he wishes or until his death.

remainder man The person who receives the remainder interest in a trust.

reserve fund An account that an organization puts its excess revenues in to cover future expenses (large or small). Both the principal and the income from the account can be spent in part or in whole as decided by the Board of Directors.

residue That part of an estate left over after all specific bequests are made and all outstanding debts are paid.

senility Loss of mental ability and memory (especially of recent events). Age related deterioration of brain cells.

settlement The transfer of property to a trust.

settlor(s) A person or group of people who transfer their ownership of some or all of their assets into a trust for the benefit of one or more people. For example, a parent or extended family that contributes to a trust for the benefit of an adult child with a developmental disability.

spendthrift trust Established to manage and administer larger assets for the benefit of a beneficiary who was deemed by the creator(s) of the trust as unable to do so for themselves.

spousal trust Established from a will for the sole benefit of the surviving spouse.

stirpes The person from whom a family or branch of a family is descended.

substitute decision-maker A person who makes decisions for an adult who is mentally incompetent to make their own decisions. The person can be limited to only financial decisions or personal care (health and long-term). *See also* ***associate decision-maker.***

support circles (*See also* ***circle***).

testamentary trust Created through a Last Will and Testament after a settlor's death. Testamentary trusts may be used to minimize income taxes by splitting income between the trust and the beneficiary. Trusts are taxed as if they were an individual for income tax purposes. Any income earned by such a trust is taxed by the same graduated tax scale as personal incomes.

three certainties To be a legal trust you must have ***certainty of intent*** (what it is intended to do), ***certainty of subject matter*** (income and capital interests clearly identified), ***certainty of objects*** (the beneficiaries clearly identified).

trust A trust is a method of contributing assets from one person to another with a person in the middle to ensure the money is well spent. A ***settlor*** transfers ownership and control of their contributed assets to a middle person, the ***trustee*** to be held in trust for the benefit of a third person or group of people, the ***beneficiaries.*** The trustee must legally manage the trust in the best interests of the beneficiaries under whatever written instructions given to them by the settlor. This relationship between trustee and beneficiaries is called ***fiduciary***, meaning the trustee holds legal title to the assets but acts in the best interests of the beneficiaries. More than one person can contribute to the trust and there can be more than one trustee. A ***testamentary trust*** is created through a person's last will and testament and takes effect upon the person's death. An ***inter vivos trust*** or ***living trust*** is a trust set up during a person's lifetime. *See also* ***precartory trust*** and ***voluntary trust.***

trust deed *See also* ***indenture.***

trustee(s) One or more people, or a trust company, entrusted with the legal ownership of assets given into a trust by settlors for the benefit of one or more other people. They administer the trust following the instructions provided by the settlor (in ***trust deed or indenture***), the courts or provincial statutes. For example, parents may choose a younger friend or colleague to act as trustee for their trust with the trust funds used to provide life-time funds to their disabled child.

voluntary trust An irrevocable trust established with the settlor as the main beneficiary. By transferring ownership of assets to the trust, the settlor protects the property and ensures some income. For example, a person that has difficulty dealing with money, may transfer ownership in their investments or in a rental property to the trust so they do not gamble the assets away.

will A legal document prepared by a person (and usually witnessed) and properly done in accordance with strict provincial laws which speaks for the person upon their death and states what they want done with their property, assets and liabilities as well as reference to guardianship issues for minor children. A will can include clauses directing the executor to create a trust fund.

Index

Note: Check the glossary for definition of terms.

Yes, I would like to offer my comments to help keep this book up-to-date.

I am a(n): O family member O friend O lawyer
O financial planner O accountant O volunteer
O member of the following organization

Please answer the following questions:

1. What did you like about the content of this book? How did it specifically help you and your family/organization?

2. Are there areas where you would have liked more or less details?

3. Are there areas that were not covered that would help other families/organizations in the future?

Name and telephone number: (optional)

Please fax, mail or e-mail your comments to:

Resources Supporting Family and Community Legacies Inc.

11 Miniot Circle, Scarborough, ON M1K 2K1 CANADA

Fax: (416) 264-4665

harry@legacies.ca

Yes, I want to help make this book available, free of charge, to other families and organizations.

Please accept my donation of:

O $20.00 O $40.00 O $60.00
O Other: ______________O Cheque enclosed

Please send my receipt to:

Name

Address

City

Province/State ________________Postal Code

Daytime telephone number:

Please mail your donation to:

The Deohaeko Support Network

400 Kingston Road

Pickering, ON L1V 6S1 CANADA

(905) 509-5654

Made in United States
North Haven, CT
11 November 2026

22197237R00153